Upton House

Warwickshire

An art gallery in a country house

In 1927 Upton House became the country home of the oil magnate and philanthropist Walter Samuel, 2nd Viscount Bearsted. Over the next 21 years, he adapted the house to display his growing art collection, which became one of the finest assembled in England in the 20th century. Inheriting his father's conventional collection of 18th-century English portraits and Dutch minor masters, Lord Bearsted started by adding English 18th-century conversation-pieces and scenes of rural life by George Stubbs. He developed an eye for the unusual and the outstanding, acquiring such touching masterpieces as Pieter Bruegel's *Death of the Virgin* and El Greco's *El Espolio*, a detail from which is illustrated on the front cover. Among the other masters represented at Upton are Holbein, Bosch, Ruisdael, Canaletto and Greuze.

The collection of 18th-century European porcelain includes Sèvres tableware and examples from most of the leading English factories, notably an unrivalled group of Chelsea figures, which is displayed in the Long Gallery.

The house was meant to be a neutral, but comfortable, background to the collections, but Lady Bearsted's silver and red bathroom has recently been revealed after restoration as one of the most striking Art Deco interiors surviving from the 1920s. On an awkward sloping site, the Bearsteds also created a garden which attractively complements the riches within the house.

When the 2nd Viscount Bearsted died in 1948, he generously bequeathed Upton House and its contents to the National Trust so that they might become that rare thing – a public art gallery of the highest quality in the depths of the countryside.

Walter Samuel, 2nd Viscount Bearsted, who created the Upton collections; by Sir John Lavery

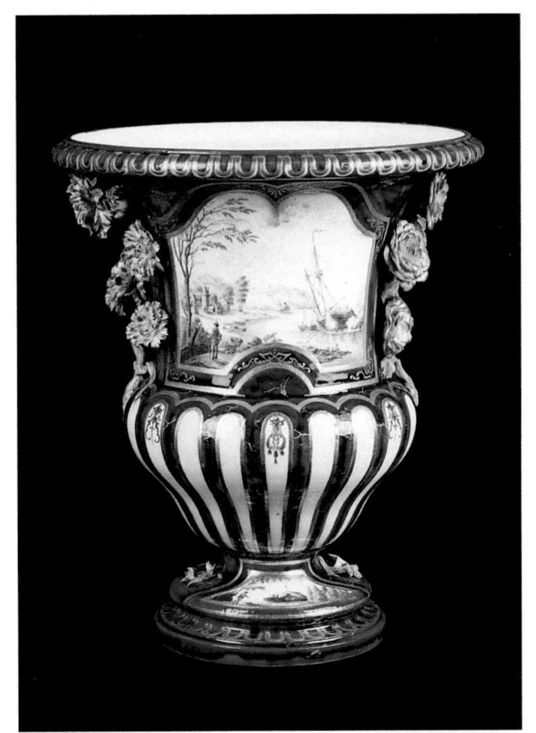

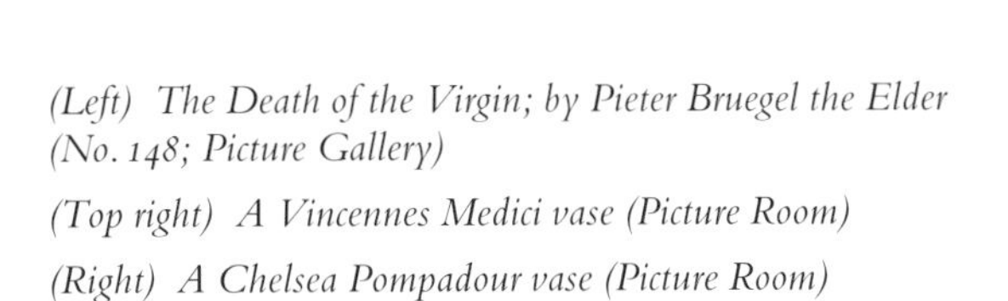

(Left) The Death of the Virgin; by Pieter Bruegel the Elder (No. 148; Picture Gallery)

(Top right) A Vincennes Medici vase (Picture Room)

(Right) A Chelsea Pompadour vase (Picture Room)

The Bearsteds at Upton *by Robert Waley-Cohen*

The purchase of Upton House

The Upton estate was purchased by Walter Samuel, 2nd Viscount Bearsted, shortly after the death of his father in 1927. He already owned Sunrising House nearby, which he had bought in 1918 as a hunting-box. He contemplated moving to The Mote, his father's house at Bearsted on the outskirts of Maidstone, Kent, but when the opportunity arose to acquire Upton, which had a common border with Sunrising, he decided to buy it, thus uniting the two estates. Besides, the foxhunting in Warwickshire was infinitely better than in Kent, and Upton was big enough to house his growing collections.

Marcus Samuel, 1st Viscount Bearsted

The man who had made it possible for Walter Samuel, 2nd Viscount Bearsted, to collect works of art so extensively and give so generously all his life was his father, Marcus Samuel, the 1st Viscount (1853–1927). Born in the East End of London in modest circumstances, Marcus Samuel was fortunate to belong to the first generation of British Jews able to play a full part in public life. In 1854, when Marcus was one year old, Jews were allowed to become Members of Parliament for the first time and in 1870 to attend university.

At the same time great commercial opportunities were opening up. During his lifetime there was a great expansion of trade with the Far East, helped by the India Act of 1833, which broke the monopoly of the East India Company, and the Treaty of Nanking, which ceded to Britain the barren rock of Hong Kong, thereby stimulating trade with China in the 1840s. Japan, too, was starting to open up after two-and-a-half centuries of isolation.

Marcus and his younger brother and business partner, Sam, who was to become a Member of Parliament, made their fortune trading with the Far East. Building on the foundations of their father's business, which had been making boxes from exotic shells brought back by sailors from the East, they developed a huge trading company, which Marcus called the Shell Transport & Trading Company, and which is known today as Royal Dutch Shell, one of the largest companies in the world.

The Samuels' first great fortune was made in the 1890s with the construction of tankers capable of passing through the Suez Canal, carrying oil in one direction and, after steam-cleaning, other goods in the opposite direction. Having developed an extensive lighting-oil business, Marcus was in a perfect position to exploit the market for oil, when this first began to replace coal in ships, and to produce petroleum for the horseless carriages powered by the internal combustion engine. By the end of the century Marcus Samuel's operations were so extensive that an observer who counted 54 ships in Yokohama harbour noted that 45 of

them belonged to, or were on charter to, Shell.

Marcus Samuel was knighted for services to the Royal Navy. He became Alderman, Sheriff and Lord Mayor of London, was made a baronet, and then raised to the peerage for his great and secret services during the First World War.

He bought The Mote in 1895 from Lord Romney, complete with contents, which included most of the full-length portraits now at Upton. The house stood in a deer-park of over 500 acres overlooking a great lake famous for its stock of coarse fish. On Marcus Samuel's death, Walter Samuel, 2nd Viscount Bearsted, decided to sell The Mote, but gave the park to the citizens of Maidstone, which now virtually surrounds it. He and his wife Dorothy had already been substantial benefactors of the Maidstone Museum, having given a collection of several thousand Japanese woodblock prints, netsuke, inro, lacquer and pottery as well as enough money to build a new wing for the Museum to house the collection.

Renovating Upton, 1927–9

In order to house the growing Bearsted collections, modernise Upton House, create enough bedrooms and add a squash court and billiard room, Lord Bearsted employed the architect Percy Morley Horder, who virtually remodelled the original 17th-century house in 1927–9. Externally the alterations at Upton included raising the one-storey wings on the garden front to the height of the main block and regularising and lengthening the entrance front, which had until then been asymmetrical. He also added at the west end at basement level the first squash court, which has now become the Picture Gallery. Internally, Morley Horder created from three rooms the 100-foot Long Gallery on the ground floor on the south front to display Lord Bearsted's collection of English soft-paste porcelain and some of his Old Master paintings. The staircase was turned round, the house was replumbed and Art Deco bathrooms added. Generally the original house was treated with tact, though the alterations give the house a strongly horizontal emphasis.

The gardens

The gardens were remodelled by Lady Bearsted under the guidance of Kitty Lloyd-Jones using the existing structure of the garden as a basis. Terraces in Hornton stone were created above the lawn on the south side of the house. The enormous laurel-covered bank which stretched from the lawn to the stone wall above the vegetable garden was made into three terraces. The staircase was created at the east end of the lawn to the bottom of the new terraces and beautiful 18th-century French bronze urns, stolen in 1976, bought for the top of the staircase. The greenhouses were moved to create the present rose garden. The Bog Garden was created out of dangerous wet ground, with the water being channelled into new surface conduits, and the sunken orchard was created out of what in 1927 was a white-tile fountain. The gardens are now one of Upton's greatest pleasures.

(Left) Marcus Samuel, 1st Viscount Bearsted; by William Orpen (Guildhall Art Gallery)

(Right) The garden front and terraces

Walter Samuel, 2nd Viscount Bearsted as collector

One of the great philanthropists of the 20th century, Walter Samuel was the benefactor of innumerable hospitals, schools, maternity homes and charitable organisations. He was also Chairman of Shell, the owner of the bankers M. Samuel (now part of Lloyds TSB) and Samuel Estates. With the merger of Bearsted maternity homes into the National Health Service, Walter Samuel is best remembered today as a passionate and knowledgeable collector.

He was a Chairman of the National Gallery, a Trustee of the Tate Gallery and from 1944 Chairman of the Whitechapel Art Gallery. Walter Samuel's greatest love was paintings but he collected over a remarkably wide range and depth in other areas. Most notably he collected tapestries, furniture, French gold boxes, English silver, English miniatures, illuminated initials, oriental works of art and European porcelain.

The parts of his collection which remain on view at Upton are outstanding in two particular fields: 18th-century soft-paste porcelain from the French and English factories, and paintings, which cover a considerable range from Hieronymus Bosch and Bruegel through El Greco and Guardi to Hogarth, Stubbs and Ben Marshall. It is a reflection of Walter Samuel's interests that almost all the pictures at Upton are concerned with human beings and their relationship with each other as well as to the world around them, while among the porcelain, figures far outnumber wares.

Even after acquiring Upton, Walter Samuel found that within ten years he had bought so many paintings that he had to convert the squash court at the west end into a picture gallery, as well as hanging paintings in the corridor leading to it. A further squash court was subsequently added at the east end of the house. On the outbreak of war in 1939, he moved out of his London residence at 1 Carlton Gardens and gave it to the Foreign Office as a suitable house for the Foreign Secretary to live in and entertain foreigners in an appropriate style (which the Foreign Secretary still does). He moved to the Dorchester Hotel for the duration of the war and afterwards to a flat in Albany, off Piccadilly, which was furnished with fine pictures and 18th-century French soft-paste porcelain as well as his 16th-century English miniatures, 18th-century French gold boxes and furniture. However, much was moved to Upton, creating intense pressure on space. The French porcelain was displayed in the lobby to the Picture Room, as was some of his collection of Chinese snuff bottles, but there was nowhere to display his Japanese netsuke. The pictures he could not find room to hang in London or Upton were stacked against the wall in his study, now the French Room, while new purchases were hidden from his less enthusiastic wife under the bed in his dressing room. By the end of his life the store-rooms in the basement were crammed with pictures, porcelain, glass and books.

(Right) Morning; by William Hogarth (No. 43; Picture Room)

A Chelsea tea service, decorated with Chinoiserie figures, c.1760 (French Room)

The gift to the National Trust

Walter Samuel was born in 1882 and thus enjoyed a secure childhood during the late Victorian era; a young man during the Edwardian era, he lived in considerable comfort and security as the eldest son of one of the richest men of his day. He was 32 at the outbreak of the First World War and served as an officer in the West Kent Yeomanry. He survived the war but his volunteer brother and both his brothers-in-law were killed in action. By the end of his life he had experienced the General Strike, the Great Depression and a second World War in which his eldest son, an officer in the Warwickshire Yeomanry, had been severely wounded. Then in his sixties, and with failing health, he had seen a government elected that looked intent on taxing the rich to extinction. The world had changed indeed.

He wanted the collections and gardens he and his wife had created and loved to be kept intact for others to enjoy for ever. So he decided to give Upton House and its gardens, and the collections in the rooms which he considered should be open to the public, to the National Trust. He added to this gift an endowment in shares of such ample size that he could never envisage that there would not be ample funds to maintain it all in the finest style. In preparation for this gift he wrote a catalogue of the pictures, which had been transferred to the Trust together with the house and gardens by the time he died in 1948 at the age of 66. His eldest son recognised that Walter Samuel had intended to give the porcelain then at Upton and so this too passed to the National Trust. After Walter Samuel's death and that of his wife Dorothy, who died within a year, many of the works of art in London were brought to Upton, though only some of these, most notably the Sèvres porcelain in the Porcelain Lobby, are on display today.

So that the house should be alive, and enjoyed by his descendants, Walter Samuel expressed the wish that the house would continue to be occupied in its entirety by the appropriate member of the family, preferably the Viscount of the day. His eldest son, the 3rd Viscount Bearsted, did so from 1948 until his death in 1986 and was a continual and generous supporter of the National Trust and its work at Upton House.

On his death the title passed to his younger brother, but the 4th Viscount decided not to move to Upton, as did his heir. The 3rd Viscount Bearsted's daughter lived with her family at Upton House from 1986 to 1988, and they have built a new house on the Upton Estate, which has remained the family's property.

The entrance front

The central seven bays of the house were built for Sir Rushout Cullen in 1695 from the local Hornton sandstone. The Warwick sandstone door-surround and giant broken segmental pediment in Clipsham stone were added later by William Bumstead, who bought the house in 1735. There are two rainwater heads on this side of the house bearing the date 1735 and the initials 'WB'.

Photographs of Upton taken in the early 20th century show an extremely irregular façade, with ugly later towers on either side of this central section. This unattractive asymmetry was rectified in 1927 by Percy Morley Horder, the architect employed by Lord Bearsted to remodel the house. He removed the towers and added substantial wings on either side, thus giving the house a distinctly horizontal feel. The high-level balustrade was carried through the whole roof line to unify old and new, while heavier glazing bars were restored to give the house a more consistent scale. But the point where old and new met was distinguished by building a high courtyard wall with gate-piers, on which were placed urns removed from the unsightly towers.

The interior

Most of the interior of the house was also remodelled in 1927–9 by Percy Morley Horder. However, it is clear from early photographs that little of the original 17th-century interior remained by this date. Morley Horder's interior schemes reinstate the feeling of the earlier period, but with a restrained opulence and a hint of Art Deco that make Upton very much a house of the 'twenties.

Many of these alterations were made to show to best advantage the magnificent collection of paintings and porcelain for which Upton is principally known.

There are no ropes at Upton to restrict your enjoyment of the treasures in this house, but you are kindly asked not to touch objects, as this seriously shortens their life and is especially damaging to paintings and fabrics.

(Top) The entrance front. The central seven bays were built in 1695. The wings were added in 1927 for Lord Bearsted

(Right) The Dining Room

Tour of the House

The Hall

The Hall was substantially altered in 1927. Originally the staircase was separated from the main hall by two pairs of columns, and the staircase itself came down close to the east wall rather than projecting out into the room as it does now. The original balusters were reused and copies made to complete the larger dimensions of the new staircase.

The stone chimneypiece in the style of William Kent probably dates from after 1735, when William Bumstead was making alterations at Upton.

Tapestries

On the walls are hung five of a set of seven mid-17th-century ***Brussels tapestries*** (the remaining two are to be seen elsewhere in the house). Woven in wool and silk, they depict the boar and stag hunts of the Emperor Maximilian I (1459–1519) and are taken from designs by the Flemish artist Bernard van Orley (*c.*1488–1541).

Furniture, stained glass and metalwork

Below the tapestries facing the main door are two ***chests***. The one on the left is German *c.*1700, while the one on the right is in the style of a 16th-century Italian *cassone* (marriage chest). The walnut ***longcase clock***, *c.*1690, is signed 'Jacobus Markwick'. In the windows are panels of Swiss-German ***stained glass***, most of which bear inscriptions and dates of the 16th and 17th centuries.

Pictures

The paintings are numbered on the frame.

1 Sir WILLIAM BEECHEY, RA (1753–1839)
Queen Charlotte (1744–1818)
Charlotte Sophia of Mecklenburg-Strelitz married

The Hall

George III in 1761 and bore him fifteen children, all but two of whom survived into adulthood. She was painted, probably in 1793, walking in the garden at Frogmore with the Round Tower of Windsor Castle in the distance.

21 ENGLISH, early 17th-century
A Lady of the Wenlock Family

22 ENGLISH, *c.*1595
Portrait of Sir John Cutts
Probably Sir John Cutts (1571/2–1646) of Childerley, Cambridgeshire.

135 ADRIAEN PIETERSZ. VAN DER VENNE (1589–1662)
Peasants Dancing
Signed and dated 1633
After moving to The Hague in 1625, van der Venne painted mainly grisailles (monochromatic painting in grey or ochre tones) like this. He was a zealous Protestant, and his grisailles are often of a moralistic nature. The barrel and upturned drinking flask in this picture suggest a condemnation of such drunken revelry.

150 Style of JAN BRUEGEL THE YOUNGER (1601–78)
A Cottage among Trees

152 Manner of JOACHIM WTEWAEL (1566–1638)
Diana and Actaeon
Wtewael was a Flemish painter much influenced by the Mannerist style then current in Italy. The incident of Actaeon surprising Diana while bathing appears almost incidental to the composition, and the classical group makes a strange contrast with the rustic Netherlands scene behind.

155 ABEL GRIMMER (active 1592–before 1619)
Peasants dancing
Signed and dated 1614
Grimmer was an Antwerp-born painter and architect who specialised in landscapes (see No. 156, Passage to Picture Gallery) and in small genre and religious subjects.

— Follower of JACOB GERRITSZ. CUYP (1594–1651/2)
Girl with a Goat

The Luggage Lobby

Here guests' luggage was delivered, while they themselves entered via the main door. On less formal occasions it became the everyday family entrance.

Furniture

The George III ***longcase clock*** was made by Kent of Saffron Walden and the marble-topped ***pier-table*** of the same date is the pair to a table in the Dining Room.

Pictures

14a ANTHONY DEVIS (1729–1816)
Upton House from the South, (?) 1803
This view of Upton was painted for a member of the Child banking family which had owned Upton since 1757. It was long thought that Devis was indulging artistic licence in placing the classical temple at the opposite end of the lake to which it stands today. An estate map of 1774, however, shows it as painted.

Three members of the Devis family painted, and there are examples of work by each of them at Upton. Anthony was the son of Arthur, the more famous portrait painter.

(Right) A Falconer; by James William Giles, 1833 (No. 28; Luggage Lobby)

23 John Ferneley (1782–1860)
A Man in Hunt Uniform
Ferneley was born and lived for most of his life in the great hunting county of Leicestershire. He was from 1801 to 1804 a pupil of Ben Marshall (No. 50, Dining Room) and is principally remembered for his paintings of hunting scenes and portraits of huntsmen and their horses.

28 James William Giles, RSA (1801–70)
A Falconer
Signed and dated 1833
Giles lived most of his life in Aberdeen where he gained a local reputation as a painter of sporting subjects. Traditionally, this picture depicts a falconer employed by the Duke of Leeds.

John Frederick Herring Senior (1795–1865)
39 *Foxhunting Scene* (A set of eight)
40 *Farmyard Scenes* (A set of eight)
Herring was an immensely popular and prosperous painter of sporting and rural subjects. These scenes are typical of his work in the 1840s. His later output is more sentimental.

47 George Henry Laporte (1799–1873)
The 13th Earl of Eglinton on Horseback
Lord Eglinton is most famous for organising the mock-medieval Eglinton tournament in 1839. The horse, according to a note on the back, is 'Emerald by Grafton', and on the frame the house in the distance is described as being Sandford Hall, Shropshire, possibly a house rented by Lord Eglinton as a hunting-box.

90 W. H. Turner (active 1849–87)
Lincoln Horse Fair
W. H. Turner specialised in painting horses – hence his nickname, 'Horsefair Turner'.

The Dining Room

This room, and a corresponding room at the west end of the house, were added either by Francis Child or his brother Robert in the late 18th century. These additions were of one storey, and their curious appearance can be seen in the view of Upton by Anthony Devis in the Luggage Lobby (No. 14a).

Furniture

The furniture is mostly 18th-century English in style. Of particular interest is the set of twelve George I-style walnut ***dining-chairs*** with seats embroidered by the 3rd Lord Bearsted. Lord

? Francis Popham; manner of Arthur Devis (No. 15; Dining Room)

Bearsted took up embroidery for therapeutic reasons after being badly injured in the Second World War. There is a stool at the far end of the Long Gallery which is also his work.

The dining- and two side-tables are all of mahogany. The cheval fire-screen contains a panel of late 18th-century Chinese silkwork depicting three herons.

Ceramics

Early Worcester porcelain from the Dr Wall period (1751–76).

Pictures

The dominant feature of the room is the fine group of English sporting paintings which reflects the keen interest of the Bearsted family in hunting.

14 RICHARD BARRETT DAVIS (1782–1854)
Thomas Sebright with the Fitzwilliam Hounds
Signed and dated 1839

Sebright was huntsman to the Fitzwilliam Hounds from 1822 to 1860. The buildings in the background are the 18th-century kennels in the park at Milton, Northamptonshire, which were designed to look like a ruined castle.

About 1760 Francis Child, who then lived at Upton, sold the majority of his hounds to Lord Fitzwilliam. The hounds in this picture are probably therefore descended from Mr Child's hounds.

15 Manner of ARTHUR DEVIS (1711–87)
? Francis Popham

Traditionally thought to show a member of the Popham family fishing in the River Kennet where it passed through the family estate at Littlecote, Wiltshire. As it was probably painted in the 1760s, it must be Francis Popham (d. 1780) who is seen here. For a portrait of his nephew, see No. 20 (Billiard Room).

50 BEN MARSHALL (1767–1835)
Francis Dukinfield Astley (1781–1835) *and his Harriers*
Signed and dated 1809

Astley of Dukinfield Hall in Cheshire was sheriff of Cheshire, 1806–7. A man of literary talents, he published in 1819 *Poems and Translations*. He kept his own pack of harriers and built the Hunter's Tower, seen in the background, on a hill overlooking Stalybridge, in 1807.

Peter Beckford's Hounds; by Francis Sartorius, 1785 (No. 70; Dining Room)

Born in Leicestershire, Marshall started life as a schoolmaster before moving to London where, from 1801, he quickly established himself as one of the leading sporting artists of the age. A mail-coach accident in 1819 forced him to give up his work as an artist, whereupon he took up sporting journalism.

FRANCIS SARTORIUS (1734–1804)

Sartorius came from a family of four generations of sporting artists. The son of John Sartorius, he was born in Nuremberg but later came to live and work in England. These pictures are typical of the concern in English sporting painting with portraying the precise appearance of animals.

70 *Peter Beckford's Hounds*
Signed and dated 1785

Peter Beckford (1740–1811) of Stepleton in Dorset was a cousin of William Beckford (No. 68, Picture Room). He was one of the first English writers to describe the science of hunting and was the author of *Thoughts upon Hunting* (1781), in which he lists the names of the hounds appearing in these paintings.

Beckford's hounds are seen with two hunt servants, who wear a livery of buff coats with black facings and carry short swords, a privilege permitted their master as a Ranger of Cranborne Chase. Several of the hounds which appear in Nos 71 and 72 are incorporated in the central picture. The one with its head down in the foreground is Belmaid and corresponds exactly to the portrait in No. 72. Other hounds which can be recognised are Guider, who leads the pack, and Mannerley (both from No. 72).

The Reapers; by George Stubbs, 1783 (No. 84; Dining Room)

71 *Two Couple of Hounds in a Park Landscape with Two Terriers*

Signed and dated 1785

The pedigree of each hound is given on the frame below.

72 *Two Couple of Hounds in a Park Landscape with Two Terriers*

Signed and dated 1785

82 Attributed to FRANCIS WHEATLEY (1747–1801)

A Man with a Gun, early 1770s

This painting has been attributed to both Stubbs and Zoffany. The present attribution is only tentative; Wheatley's early paintings are small-scale portraits in the manner of Zoffany and Mortimer.

GEORGE STUBBS, ARA (1724–1806)

83 *The Haymakers*

Signed and dated 1783

Stubbs is popularly thought of as a painter of animals, particularly racehorses, but in the 1780s he painted several farming scenes, of which this painting, and its companion (No. 84), are outstanding, albeit damaged, examples. Stubbs treats his subject in an unsentimental way and has obviously observed each activity closely.

84 *The Reapers*

Signed and dated 1783

Companion to No. 83.

This painting is very thinly painted on wooden panels in Stubbs's characteristically fragile medium, a mixture of beeswax and pine resin, with only a little oil. It has suffered in the last 200 years, and the horizontal joins between the panels are clearly visible.

85 *The Labourers*

Signed and dated 1779

Also known as *Lord Torrington's Bricklayers at Southill,* this painting was one of a series of three commissioned pictures showing the outdoor servants and workmen at Torrington's estate at Southill, Bedfordshire. Ozias Humphry, a painter and Stubbs's long-time friend, recorded the following story about the painting of this picture: 'Mr Stubbs was a long time loitering about observing the old Men without perceiving any thing that engaged them all so as to make a fit subject for a picture till at length they fell into a dispute about the manner of putting the Tail piece into the Cart which dispute so favorable for his purpose lasted long enough for him to make a sketch of the picture Men, Horse and Cart as they have been represented.' This anecdote shows us that Stubbs's country scenes were the result of the close observation of men and women at work in the countryside.

91 THOMAS WEAVER (1774–1843)
John Corbet and the Warwickshire Foxhounds
Signed and dated 1812

It is appropriate that this painting should be in the collection of a family so closely associated with the Warwickshire Hunt. John Corbet of Sundorne Castle, Shropshire, is regarded as the founder of the Warwickshire, of which he became Master in 1791. The Warwickshire hounds were known as 'The Sons of Trojan', taking their name from a famous hound in the pack said to be represented as the leading hound in this picture. In 1812 Corbet was succeeded as master by the 6th Lord Middleton, who paid 1,200 guineas for the pack. The fact that the picture is dated 1812 and was in the collection of Lord Middleton, may imply that it was commissioned as a portrait to commemorate Corbet's association with the Warwickshire hounds.

The Long Gallery

The Long Gallery was created from several smaller rooms in the alterations of 1927–9. Here the paintings are nearly all 16th- and 17th-century Dutch, and the porcelain, in cabinets along the right-hand wall, is English 18th-century (see p. 18).

Furniture

The furniture is mainly 18th-century English in style. The large set of gilt seat furniture incorporates late 18th-century French tapestry scenes after François Boucher.

Textiles

In a frame in the central part of the Long Gallery are two panels of 17th-century ***French needle-work*** from a book cover.

Ceramics

At the far end of the room, standing on a Japanese black lacquer cabinet with an early 18th-century gilt stand, is a large Chinese ceramic horse of the Tang dynasty (AD 618–906). Known as Mingqi, these horses and other

The Long Gallery

earthenware figures were buried in great numbers as part of the funeral rites of important people. After firing, these figures were brightly painted, but little of this paint remains today.

Photographs

The photographs are of the 2nd Lord Bearsted (in uniform), who formed the collections, his son, the 3rd Lord Bearsted, and his daughter, the Hon. Mrs Robert Waley-Cohen, and her family.

Pictures

111 JAN VAN DE CAPPELLE (*c.*1624/5–79)
A River Estuary
Jan van de Cappelle was a prosperous dyer in Amsterdam, who taught himself to paint in his spare time. He was a marine specialist concerned with the atmosphere of sea, sky and clouds; his works create an exquisite sense of calm. He amassed a large art collection which included works by Rubens and Van Dyck, as well as over 500 drawings by Rembrandt. His portrait was painted by Rembrandt and Frans Hals.

112 COLOGNE SCHOOL, 1650
Anna Maria Mockel as a Child
Of the two coats of arms in this picture, the one on the left is that of the Mockel family of Westphalia.

113 COLOGNE SCHOOL, 1650
A Younger Brother of Anna Maria Mockel
Pair to No. 112. Formerly catalogued as by Jacob Gerritsz. Cuyp, the father of Aelbert Cuyp, but it is now thought to be by a close imitator. It is the portrait of a little boy, still too young to be in trousers.

114 MELCHIOR DE HONDECOETER (1636–95)
A Turkey Cock and other Birds in a Garden
Signed and dated 1672
Hondecoeter came from an artistic family; both his father and uncle were painters. He worked in The Hague and Amsterdam and specialised in pictures of bird fights, birds in flight, and still-lifes with birds and game.

115 Attributed to GOVERT FLINCK (1615–60)
A Child holding a Dog
Flinck was a pupil of Rembrandt and initially attempted to follow his master's style. This picture was probably painted in the 1640s, but gives little indication of any debt to Rembrandt.

116 After WILLEM CORNELISZ. DUYSTER (*c.*1599–1635)
The Interior of a Barn with an Officer
Duyster was a painter of interiors, and musical and guard groups. There is a better version of this painting in the Mauritshuis in The Hague, which suggests that this is a contemporary copy.

117 JAN VAN GOYEN (1596–1656)
A River Scene
Signed and dated 1643
Van Goyen was born in Leyden where he studied under Esaias van de Velde. His early landscapes share van de Velde's sense of colour, but after about 1630 he developed this near-monochromatic style with a dominance of brown tones. The incidents are all subordinate to the tonality, which results in a pervasive sense of stillness.

119 JOHANNES JANSON (1729–84)
A Winter Landscape
Signed
Janson was a Dutch painter and etcher but was born in the East Indies, coming to Holland only at the age of eight. Although at first an engineer, he soon

turned to painting, mainly landscapes and pictures of cattle in the style of Paulus Potter.

121 JOHANNES VAN HAENSBERGEN (1642–1705)
A Classical Landscape with Women bathing
This painting was formerly thought to be by Cornelis van Poelenburgh (the bogus initials C. P. are prominent on one of the rocks), but it is almost certainly by his pupil, Haensbergen. The general style of the two painters is similar, and both belonged to the so-called Italianate Dutch school. Landscapes by these artists have a distinctly Italian atmosphere, although they are nearly always imaginary.

122 EMANUEL MEURANT (1622–1700)
A Landscape with Cottages
Bears a false signature of Paulus Potter and the date 1646

A Dutch landscape painter and pupil of Wouwerman, Meurant none the less painted a number of landscapes in the manner of Potter.

127 GUILLAM DUBOIS (*c.*1610–80)
A Country Road
Bears a false monogram of Salomon van Ruysdael and a date of 1636

Previously accepted as a work of Salomon van Ruysdael on the strength of the monogram, this painting is now thought to be an early work by Dubois.

128 PIETER JANSZ. SAENREDAM (1597–1665)
The Interior of the Church of St Catherine, Utrecht
Saenredam was a Haarlem artist who specialised in painting church interiors. His works are very austere; the people in them are small and seem to be included only to give a sense of scale to the architecture. Those

(Left) Anna Maria Mockel as a Child; Cologne School, 1650 (No. 112; Long Gallery)

(Right) The Interior of the Church of St Catherine, Utrecht; by Pieter Jansz. Saenredam (No. 128; Long Gallery)

English porcelain in the Long Gallery

In the four wall cabinets in the Long Gallery is a large collection of early English porcelain from the Chelsea, Bow, Derby, Worcester and Liverpool factories. These are mostly figures; English tableware may be seen on the first floor.

Soft-paste and hard-paste porcelain

Most English porcelain of the 18th century is known as soft-paste. This differentiates it from true Chinese porcelain, known in Europe as hard-paste, which is made using kaolin, a soft white clay, and petuntse (feldspar), a china stone. The formula for hard-paste porcelain was unknown outside China until its discovery in Germany at the royal factory at Meissen in Saxony in 1708. The secret was closely guarded, and other European factories were forced to develop formulas using such ingredients as glass and bone in an attempt to achieve the same translucent white quality as true porcelain. Hard-paste should not, however, be thought of as superior, for both hard- and soft-paste porcelain have their individual qualities.

Chelsea

Red anchor, 1752–8

The earliest known porcelain to be made in Chelsea dates from 1745. A small factory was started in Lawrence Street under the patronage of William, Duke of Cumberland, and his secretary, Sir Everard Fawkener, but it was not until the silversmith Nicholas Sprimont became manager in 1749 that high-quality tablewares and figures were produced. Chelsea focused on making porcelain for the wealthiest and most fashionable members of society. Pieces made between 1752 and 1758 are marked with a red anchor.

Gold anchor, 1758–69

On Fawkener's death in 1758, Sprimont became both proprietor and manager. Upton possesses an unrivalled collection of figures from the gold anchor period. Profuse gilding of fine quality, richly brocaded costumes and clumps of flowers and foliage are characteristic of these boldly modelled figures.

The Music Lesson, Chelsea Gold Anchor, c.1765 (cabinet B, third shelf). Based on a design by François Boucher

William Shakespeare, Chelsea-Derby, c.1775 (cabinet D, fourth shelf). Based on Scheemakers's monument in Poets' Corner, Westminster Abbey

Two 'Mansion House' Dwarfs, Derby, c.1790 (cabinet D, third shelf). They are named after two dwarfs who stood outside the Mansion House in London displaying advertisements (painted on their hats)

Chelsea-Derby and Derby

In 1769 failing health forced Sprimont to sell the Chelsea factory. It was briefly in the hands of James Cox, but in 1770 was bought by William Duesbury, the proprietor of the Derby factory. The Derby factory had been producing porcelain since 1750 and had made figures and other porcelain in Chelsea styles. Pieces coming from the Chelsea factory under Duesbury's management are known as Chelsea-Derby (1770–83). Duesbury finally closed the Chelsea works in 1783 and moved moulds, ovens and plant to Derby.

Most of the portrait figures in Cabinet D are Derby, as are the biscuit (unglazed) porcelain pieces. These last often cost more than the coloured versions, owing to the greater care which had to be taken in finishing them.

Bow

The Bow factory in the East End of London operated from about 1746 until 1774. It was a large factory producing more everyday wares than Chelsea. The formula for Bow porcelain incorporated a large amount of bone ash, added to give strength during firing, but useful wares tended to stain brown. Figure subjects were often copies of Meissen, although some lively original work was done.

Liverpool

From the mid-1750s there were half-a-dozen or so porcelain factories in Liverpool, and it is only recently that their interrelated histories have been disentangled. They produced mainly blue-and-white tableware, but also figures and vases.

Worcester

The Worcester Porcelain Factory was formed in 1751 by Dr John Wall and fourteen partners. The factory developed a recipe for porcelain using soapstone from the Lizard, Cornwall. This produced wares less likely to crack or craze when used for hot liquids. So the factory concentrated on making tea and other useful wares, leaving the Chelsea and Derby factories to make figure subjects.

Early Worcester decoration is simple, often in Chinese style, but after 1768 painters from the Chelsea factory were employed. They brought with them a repertoire of Meissen- and Sèvres-inspired designs; this is the period of the famous underglaze scale blue grounds and overglaze exotic birds.

From the Long Gallery proceed to the Library. The Staircase Lobby is described after the Library.

Henry Woodward as 'The Fine Gentleman' and Kitty Clive as 'The Fine Lady' in Garrick's farce Lethe; *Bow, c.1750–2 (cabinet D, fourth shelf). Coloured examples of these figures are very rare*

here were probably the work of another artist, Isaak van Nickelen (active *c.*1660–d. 1703), one of Saenredam's pupils.

Saenredam painted relatively few pictures. This dates from the 1660s, but was worked up from a drawing made during a visit to Utrecht in 1636.

129 Attributed to GODFRIED SCHALCKEN (1643–1706)
Boys flying Kites
Schalcken was a painter of portraits and genre scenes. He was a pupil of Gerrit Dou and specialised in artificially lit scenes.

JAN STEEN (1625/6–79)
131 *The Sense of Hearing*
132 *The Sense of Taste*
133 *The Sense of Smell*
134 *The Sense of Sight*
All signed
These four pictures come from a group of five illustrating the Five Senses. The *Sense of Touch* is missing.

Steen is principally known for his paintings of low life such as tavern scenes (he himself ran a brewery), but in which there is always a strong moral sense. A pitcher stands beside each peasant and each seems somewhat the worse for drink. Though Steen was a keen observer of mankind, his technique has a sketchy, free quality.

The Sense of Sight; by Jan Steen (No. 134; Long Gallery)

136 PHILIPS WOUWERMAN (1619–68)
A Landscape with Dunes and Figures
Signed
Wouwerman was a Haarlem artist who is chiefly known for dramatic landscapes such as this. The low viewpoint adopted by the artist throws the trees and animals into silhouette against the stormy sky. Artists like Wouwerman and Jacob van Ruisdael (No. 126, Passage to the Picture Gallery) were reacting against the tonal calm of, for example, such pictures as No. 117 by van Goyen in this room.

Style of JAN BRUEGEL the Elder (1568–1625)
172 *A Harbour Scene*
173 *A Village Scene*
Purchased as a pair by Lord Bearsted in 1922, Nos 172 and 173 are clearly by different artists, No. 172 being of a higher quality.

The Library

The Library was created for the 2nd Viscount Bearsted by Morley Horder as part of the 1927–9 remodelling of the house. The interpenetration of spaces, created by the balcony overlooking the Picture Room, relates more to the Modern Movement influenced by Frank Lloyd Wright, than to the traditional English country house. The balcony, which was removed as part of alterations made for the 3rd Viscount, was restored when the Picture Room was reinstated in 1994.

Pictures

24 THOMAS GAINSBOROUGH, RA (1727–88)
Crossing the Ford
This is thought to be Gainsborough's earliest surviving landscape. It dates from the late 1740s, just after he had returned to his native Suffolk from London.

42 WILLIAM HOGARTH (1697–1764)
Gerard Anne Edwards (1732–73) *in his Cradle*
Known in later life as 'Handsome Edwards', he was the son of Lord Anne Hamilton and Mary Edwards, the richest heiress in England, who repudiated her marriage and had him baptised as her son alone.

Crossing the Ford; by Thomas Gainsborough (No. 24; Library)

The photographs are of the 3rd Lord Bearsted and his family.

Porcelain

Among the other objects in the room is a 19th-century Sèvres figure of Marie Antoinette in biscuit porcelain.

The Picture Room, seen from the balcony, is described on p. 27. Return to the Staircase Lobby.

The Staircase Lobby

Pictures

17 ARTHUR DEVIS (1711–87)
Mr and Mrs Van Harthals and their Son
Signed and dated 1749
Mr Van Harthals was a Dutch merchant living at Gravesend. The view may therefore be of the Thames estuary.

56 JOHN OPIE, RA (1761–1807)
A Country Girl
On his arrival in London in 1781 Opie was heralded as the 'Cornish Wonder', an untutored prodigy whose portraits of peasants, children and old people showed a Rembrandtesque handling of light and deep shade. Reynolds was moved to pronounce: 'Ah! There is such a young man come out of Cornwall ... like Caravaggio, but finer!' This painting was exhibited at the Royal Academy in 1795. Despite some decline in his artistic powers, Opie was constantly admired, and he was elected RA in 1787 and Professor of Painting in 1795.

63 Sir HENRY RAEBURN, RA (1756–1823)
*The Macdonald Children, c.*1800
The eldest boy, Reginald (or Ranald), sits on the right, with his arm about his brother Robert. The youngest boy, Donald, gazes up at them, clasping his dog in his arms. Ranald (1788–1873) succeeded as 19th Chief of Clanranald and 7th of Benbecula at the age of five, but financial difficulties later in life forced him to sell his estates. Both his brothers died unmarried in middle age.

The Macdonald Children; by Sir Henry Raeburn (No. 63; Staircase Lobby)

69 Francis Sartorius (1734–1804)
A Man on Horseback

253 Imitator of Francisco de Goya (1746–1828)
Don Francisco Bayeu y Subias (1734–95)
Bayeu was a Spanish painter, and Goya's master and brother-in-law. Despite this personal connection, this portrait is now thought to be a pastiche of a genuine portrait of Bayeu painted by Goya in 1786. It follows the composition of the authentic work, but with a handling of paint that Goya was not to develop until after Bayeu's death.

From the Staircase Lobby, proceed down the stairs to the Porcelain Lobby.

The Lower Staircase

Pictures

41 Joseph Highmore (1692–1780)
Isaac Welman
Signed and dated 1737
Welman, of Poundisford Park near Taunton, is shown as a young man of 26. The volume of Pope's poetry in his hand suggests that he had literary interests. Highmore was a popular portrait painter in the mid-18th century. Among his most famous works are his twelve illustrations to Samuel Richardson's novel *Pamela* which have a Rococo elegance.

59 Philip Reinagle (1749–1833)
*Three Children dressing up, c.*1788
Reinagle's portraits are less well-known than his hunting scenes. Once thought to represent his own three children, it was exhibited at the RA in 1788 simply titled *Portraits of Three Children.*

77 Robert Smirke, RA (1752–1845)
A Scene from 'The Busybody'
The Busybody was a comedy by Mrs Centlivre (born Susanna Carroll), an actress and dramatist who married Queen Anne's chef. It was first produced in 1709. The episode illustrated takes place in Act IV, Scene II, when Isabinda pretends to faint in order to prevent her father, Sir Jealous Traffick, from opening the cupboard in which her lover is hiding. Her servant, Patch, is kneeling beside her, feigning concern.

The Porcelain Lobby

Pictures

12 John Constable, RA (1776–1837)
Harnham Ridge, near Salisbury
Constable made oil sketches like this one from nature and later worked some of them up into finished pictures in his studio. Today these sketches, with their free brushwork, are often preferred to the more polished final versions which he exhibited at the Royal Academy. This sketch was probably painted at Salisbury in 1828.

35 Attributed to George Henry Harlow (1787–1819)
'Mrs Fitzwilliam'
Nothing is known of Mrs Fitzwilliam. Harlow was at one time a pupil of the great portrait painter Sir Thomas Lawrence (No. 48). This permitted him 'to have access to Sir Thomas's house at nine o'clock in the morning, with leave to copy his pictures till four o'clock in the afternoon, but to receive no instruction of any kind.' For this he paid 100 guineas a year. Such was the tuition in a successful artist's studio! Harlow built himself a successful career as a portrait and historical painter but was never admitted to the Royal Academy, having parted company with Lawrence on bad terms.

92 ? Robert West (d. 1770)
Thomas Smith and his Family
Signed *R. West* and dated 1733
Smith was a Frenchman whose original name was Le Fevre. The family's only claim to fame, according to a note on the reverse, was that one of his grandsons married the Duke of Wellington's sister. The attribution is only tentative. West was an Irish artist who, after studying in Paris, started the first School of Design in Dublin. He was, however, principally a draughtsman, and this would be his only known painting.

98 Richard Wilson, RA (1714–82)
A Convent on a Rock
This is one of five versions by Wilson of this subject which represents a view in Italy, probably imaginary. Wilson was the first major British artist to concentrate on landscape. His style was much influenced by a stay in Italy, 1750–7, and the works of Claude Lorrain and Gaspard Poussin.

Sèvres in the Porcelain Lobby

Experimental workshops were set up in the royal château of Vincennes south of Paris by 1738–40, and the factory was in regular production by 1745. In 1756 the factory moved to Sèvres, having outgrown its premises. Louis XV bought the factory outright in 1759, having granted the Vincennes factory fourteen years previously the French monopoly on producing porcelain wares with coloured and gilded decoration. All Vincennes/Sèvres porcelain is soft-paste, if it was made before the late 1770s; after this date, both hard- and soft-paste wares were made at Sèvres until 1800, when production of soft-paste ceased.

A coffee cup and saucer, 1778, from the service commissioned by Catherine the Great of Russia. It was one of the most lavish ever produced at Sèvres (cabinet G, top shelf)

Most of the production at Sèvres was devoted to wares rather than figures. Responsibility for shapes was largely in the hands of Jean-Claude Duplessis, artistic director, 1748–74. He also decided which areas of the pieces should be covered with ground colours. There are six ground colours: *bleu lapis*, a dark blue underglaze ground found on early pieces, after 1751; *bleu nouveau*, a dark blue overglaze ground which replaced *bleu lapis* after 1763; *bleu céleste*, a turquoise ground, derived from imported Chinese wares, first used in 1753; *rose*, a pink ground, after 1757; *vert*, green, first recorded in 1752; yellow, early pieces from 1753 are richer than those of the 1780s and '90s.

Painting in panels reserved on these grounds is a characteristic of much Sèvres porcelain. The choice of subject, as well as other painted decoration, was the responsibility of the second artistic director, Jean-Jacques Bachelier, 1748/51–93. Common subjects were scenes of children after the painter François Boucher, harbour scenes by Morin, while flowers were painted by, among others, Prévost.

The production of Sèvres wares was a time-consuming process. Even the simplest piece in a grand service, such as a plate, passed through the hands of at least eight specialist craftsmen: the

A wine cooler, 1792, from a service commissioned by Louis XVI for his dining room at Versailles (cabinet E, third shelf)

A bleu céleste tray, 1761, painted with a peasant scene in the manner of David Teniers

A plate made and painted for Madame du Barry, Louis XV's last mistress. She died in 1774, but it was not gilded until after 1795 (cabinet I, bottom shelf)

A bleu céleste double jardinière, 1779

moulder, the *répareur*, the glaze painter, the ground artist, the painter of flowers, the painter of cameos, the gilder and the burnisher. And after each major process, except the last, the plate had to be fired. At any stage during this process a piece might be rejected for the slightest imperfection, so it is not surprising that grand services took many years to complete. Craftsmen attained great skill, and the work of many of them can be identified by their marks.

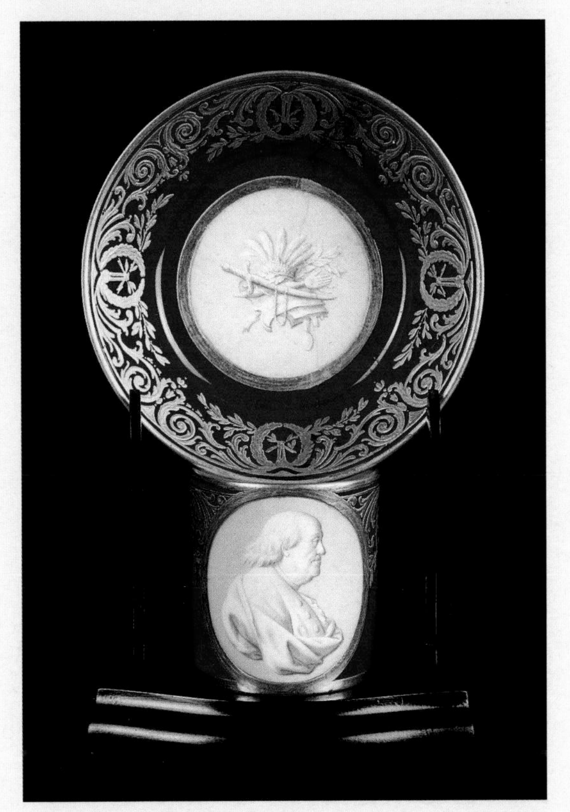

A coffee cup and saucer, decorated with a portrait of Benjamin Franklin, who was US ambassador to France, 1776–85 (cabinet H, third shelf)

The Picture Room

The Picture Room

This room was created in 1927 as a double-storey picture gallery. It was altered to a single-storey form with a drawing room above for the 3rd Lord Bearsted and restored to its earlier form in 1994. With a ceiling height of 30 feet it provides an ideal setting for the display of the large English portraits in the collection. Off this room is the panelled Inglenook and the Billiard Room, with the Library above the latter.

Furniture

Among the furniture is a Regency ***rosewood table*** in the manner of Robert le Gaigneur, with inlaid brass banding and scrolling. The set of four mahogany side-chairs is early George III in date.

Ceramics

On a table in the Inglenook stands a ***Chinese pottery figure of a winged mythical beast*** from the T'ang dynasty. Later tomb figures were often splashed glazed in this way.

Pictures

16 ARTHUR DEVIS (1711–87)
The Edgar Children
Signed and dated 1762
Elizabeth and Charlotte Edgar of Red House Park, Ipswich. The younger of the two, Charlotte, was born in 1757 and married General François Lewis Hugonin, in whose family this painting remained until 1929, when it was acquired by Lord Bearsted.
It is typical of Devis's painting and a good example of the 'conversation-piece' popular in England in the mid-18th century, in which a small-scale group would be seen 'conversing' in what was thought to be a natural and informal manner.

WILLIAM HOGARTH (1697–1764)
Hogarth was the most important English artist of the first half of the 18th century. He did more than anyone to rid English art of its dependence on foreign models and styles.

43 *Morning*
This, and its pair (No. 44), were once part of a set of four paintings entitled *The Four Times of the Day*. The four were split up when Hogarth auctioned the paintings in 1745. The Upton pair was bought by Sir William Heathcote, in whose family they remained until acquired by Lord Bearsted in 1938. The other two, *Afternoon and Evening,* were bought by the Duke of Ancaster, with whose descendants they remain.

Morning is set in Covent Garden, where an old spinster, dressed in yellow, is making her way to early morning service at St Paul's church. The once-grand square has become less popular with the nobility, following the expansion of the vegetable market, and taverns have opened. The young men have probably spent the night carousing and are now pressing their attentions on some market girls. In front of them some poor people try to warm themselves by a fire; one of them extends a begging hand to the old maid. Her failure to notice this, or the cold suffered by her page boy, is a criticism of her Christian charity.

44 *Night*
Another sordid scene of London life. It takes place in a street off Charing Cross. Although it is night,

(Right) Night; by William Hogarth (No. 44; Picture Room)

everyone is awake except the tramps under the barber's window. In this upside-down world a man is being shaved at night. A carriage has overturned after its horses have shied at a bonfire lit beside the road. In the foreground a drunken Freemason is being escorted home, and at the end of the street a cart passes loaded high with household belongings: tenants doing a moonlight flit.

64 Sir HENRY RAEBURN, RA (1756–1823)
The 13th Earl of Eglinton (1812–61)

The young Earl, Archibald, is seen aged about ten on horseback in front of Eglinton Castle (see also No. 47, Luggage Lobby). With his fluid, painterly technique, Raeburn established himself as the leading Scottish portrait painter of his day and the equal of his London rivals.

66 Sir JOSHUA REYNOLDS, PRA (1723–92)
The Earl and Countess of Ely

Henry Loftus (1709–83) was created Earl of Ely in 1771. He is shown here with his second wife, Anne, whom he married in 1775. The portrait was probably commissioned to celebrate that event.

68 GEORGE ROMNEY (1734–1802)
William Beckford (1760–1844)

Beckford inherited a huge fortune from his father and built the vast mock-Gothic mansion Fonthill Abbey, designed by James Wyatt, which he filled with superb and varied collections of Old Masters and works of art. He also wrote the Gothic romance, *Vathek, An Arabian Tale*. After a homosexual scandal involving the young 'Kitty' Courtenay, he lived as a recluse. Romney's career overlapped those of Reynolds and Gainsborough. After a visit to Italy in 1773–5, he attempted history paintings in the grand manner, but he was never successful in this genre. In his portraits he is at his best. However, he died insane, with a deep sense of artistic failure.

81 THOMAS STOTHARD (1755–1834)
George III and his Family

This group portrait, painted in 1787, shows the King and Queen seated, surrounded by members of their family.

Studio of Sir ANTHONY VAN DYCK (1599–1641)

Van Dyck was a Flemish painter, whose fame in England rests largely on the portraits of King Charles I and his court painted after 1632, when he was appointed court painter. Like most successful artists of the day, Van Dyck ran a large studio, and many works formerly attributed to him are now known to be studio productions. These two portraits are typical of the elegant style which Van Dyck developed after a visit to Italy in 1622–6, and which had such an influence on English portrait painting right through to the end of the 19th century.

169 *Queen Henrietta Maria* (1609–69)

The wife of Charles I. She was the youngest daughter of Henry IV of France and Marie de' Medici, and the sister of Louis XIII.

170 *Margaret of Lorraine* (1613–72)

The daughter of Francis, Count of Vaudémont, and sister of Charles, 3rd Duke of Lorraine. In 1632 she married Gaston d'Orléans, the younger son of Henry IV and Marie de' Medici; she was thus sister-in-law to Queen Henrietta Maria (No. 169)

Sir HUBERT VON HERKOMER, RA (1849–1914)

Herkomer was born in Bavaria, but in 1857 his family settled in Britain, where he became popular for his sober portraits.

Sir Marcus Samuel, Bt, later 1st Viscount Bearsted (1853–1927)
Signed and dated 1908
Marcus Samuel founded Shell Transport & Trading Company Ltd.

Fanny, Lady Samuel, later Viscountess Bearsted
Signed and dated 1909
Wife of Marcus Samuel.

Porcelain

On either side of the entrance to the Billiard Room are cabinets containing French porcelain from the Sèvres and Vincennes factories.

The Billiard Room

Pictures

5 Attributed to LUKE CLENNELL (1781–1840)
A Village Fair

13 NATHANIEL DANCE, RA (1735–1811)
William Weddell and William Palgrave
Signed and dated 1765
Weddell was in Italy in 1765–6, where he was painted by Dance. Weddell, like many gentlemen doing the Grand Tour, bought numerous works of art, which he displayed at his home, Newby Hall, near Ripon, which was remodelled for him by Robert Adam. Weddell made the Tour with the Rev. William Palgrave, a friend of the poet Thomas Gray. Weddell's servant is, by tradition, named Janson.

20 ARTHUR WILLIAM DEVIS (1762–1822)
Edward William Leyborne-Popham (1764–1843)
He succeeded to the estates of Littlecote, Ramsbury and Houndstrete Park on the death in 1780 of his uncle, Francis Popham, who is probably portrayed in No. 15 (Dining Room). He was painted, probably in 1788, in the uniform of an officer of the Light Company of the 24th (or 2nd Warwickshire Regiment of Foot). Leyborne, who rose to the rank of general, took the additional name and arms of Popham in 1805. Arthur William Devis was the son of Arthur Devis. He was both a portrait and historical painter and spent ten years in India. He died of a fit of apoplexy in 1822.

49 RICHARD LIVESAY (1753–*c.*1823)
The Duchess of York presented to George III
Queen Charlotte is presenting Frederica, eldest daughter of Frederick William II of Prussia, to George III. The occasion is the princess's marriage to Frederick, Duke of York, who stands on the right of the picture. Behind the King and Queen are the Prince of Wales and, right, the Duke of Clarence. On the left are the royal princesses. Livesay was, from 1790 to 1793, drawing master to the children of George III at Windsor. He was a pupil-assistant of Benjamin West.

(Left) William Beckford; by George Romney (No. 68; Picture Room)

(Right) William Weddell and William Palgrave; by Nathaniel Dance, 1765 (No. 13; Billiard Room)

54 John Hamilton Mortimer, ARA (1741–79)
The Rev. Charles Everard Booth, DD, and Capt. Griffith Booth, RN, playing Billiards
Billiards is one of the few indoor games that is well documented in art. In this case it provides a conversation-piece setting for a portrait. The Rev. Charles Everard is seated on the left with his nephew, Capt. Griffith Booth, standing in the centre; a marker on the right holds a mace, the precursor of the billiard cue. The picture probably shows the billiard room at Twemlow Hall in Cheshire *c.*1770.

55 Alexander Nasmyth (1758–1840)
The 7th Baron Belhaven (1765–1814)
He was born William Hamilton of Wishaw in Lanarkshire. The house in the distance is almost certainly the Hamiltons' seat at Wishaw, which was demolished in the 1950s. In 1789 William married Penelope Macdonald, who was the aunt of the boys shown in Raeburn's *Macdonald Children* (No. 63, Staircase Lobby).

Nasmyth was primarily a landscape painter, but before travelling to Italy in 1782–4 he had established himself as a portrait painter in Edinburgh. This portrait dates from his return to Scotland.

The Artist in his Studio; by Richard Morton Paye (No. 57; Billiard Room)

57 Richard Morton Paye (1750–1821)
The Artist in his Studio
Paye was a painter of portraits, miniatures and genre subjects, especially of children, as well as an engraver. He began his career as an engraver of silver and a wax modeller. Although at first very successful, he later fell into extreme poverty. He exhibited this painting at the Royal Academy in 1783 under the title of *An Engraver at Work*. It is in fact a portrait of himself engraving Nathaniel Dance's portrait of Dr Percival Pott, who gave his name to an operation to set a fractured ankle, a method still used today.

60 Anglo-Dutch, *c.*1745
A Lady winding Wool and a Gentleman drawing
Previously catalogued as the work of Arthur Pond, this painting has also been associated with Pieter van Bleek (1697–1764), a Dutch painter who had settled in England by 1723.

Return to the Porcelain Lobby and go down the stairs to the Passage to the Picture Gallery.

The Passage to the Picture Gallery

Furniture and sculpture

On the marble-topped giltwood side-table in the style of William Kent stands a bronze statue of a horse by A. L. Wental.

Pictures

118 Jan van der Heyden (1637–1712)
Farm Buildings seen through an Archway
Van der Heyden is principally known as a painter of townscapes. Born in Gorinchem, he moved to Amsterdam where he became the first artist in that city to paint such scenes. There is a precision in his handling of buildings which is seen here in the minute detailing of the ruined arch. He was also a designer of fire-engines and street lighting.

120 Gabriel Metsu (1629–67)
The Duet ('Le Corsage Bleu')
The lute and musical score are symbols of love and courtship, which may be the subject of this picture.

Metsu was a Dutch painter, mainly of genre subjects and interiors. Although he was the pupil of Gerrit Dou, his work has a delicacy closer to that of Pieter de Hooch and sometimes even Vermeer.

123 Attributed to JAN LIEVENS (1607–74)
A Priest at an Altar

This is one of several versions of this composition. Despite an apparent signature by Rembrandt, the Upton version is now thought to be by Jan Lievens, a contemporary of Rembrandt in Leyden. The two painters were closely associated in the 1620s and their early work is often confused.

125 Follower of REMBRANDT VAN RIJN (1606–69)
An Unknown Woman

Rembrandt became the most fashionable portrait painter in the Netherlands following his move to Amsterdam in 1632. He ran a large studio and was much copied, and for this reason experts have doubted the authenticity of many paintings formerly ascribed to him. Were it to be genuine, the style of No. 125 would suggest it was painted about 1634.

126 JACOB VAN RUISDAEL (1628/9–82)
Le Coup de Soleil
Signed

A view from the dunes of Overveen looking towards the city of Haarlem, with the Grote Kerk standing out on the horizon.

(Above) The Duet; by Gabriel Metsu (No. 120; Passage to Picture Gallery)

(Right) Le Coup de Soleil; by Jacob van Ruisdael (No. 126; Passage to Picture Gallery)

Ruisdael is considered the greatest Dutch landscape artist of the 17th century. His paintings of rushing torrents and gnarled trees influenced the early romantics of the 19th century, but perhaps his best pictures are of the type of Dutch landscape seen here. It is still a dramatic scene: the sun is breaking through a large stormy sky, illuminating the fields in the middle distance, but the light serves only to emphasise the melancholy power of the massive clouds.

130 JAN STEEN (1626–79)
The Tired Traveller
Signed
The title is, like that of many Dutch genre paintings, a 19th-century invention. It gives misleading sentimental overtones to what is basically a humorous and critical view of life. The scene is a tavern, and the cut flower, symbolising the short-lived nature of physical beauty and love, hints at lascivious thoughts.

156 ABEL GRIMMER (1573–?1619)
Four Scenes from a Series of the Months
Three signed
Previously described as *The Four Seasons,* but more likely to have come from a set of twelve paintings representing the months. A set of twelve larger roundels by Grimmer has similar scenes from which we may deduce the following: (1) *Woodcutters* – February; (2) *Sheep shearing* – June; (3) *Haymakers* – July; (4) *A Town Scene under Snow* – January.

163 FRANS POURBUS THE YOUNGER (1569–1622)
Martin Ruzé (1529–1616)
Signed and dated 1612
Ruzé was a French statesman who served Henry III, first as Financial Secretary and in 1588 as Secretary of State. Under Henry IV he was made Grand Treasurer of the Orders of the King of France. As the inscription indicates, Ruzé was 83 when this portrait was painted. Pourbus the Younger was a thorough professional, travelling the courts of Europe painting royalty and nobility. This portrait was painted while he was in Paris, where, from 1610, he was court painter to Marie de' Medici and, later, to Anne of Austria.

166 After Sir PETER PAUL RUBENS (1577–1640)
Judas Maccabaeus praying for the Dead
This painting is probably a copy of a lost sketch by Rubens for his altarpiece in Tournai Cathedral (*c.*1618–20), which is now in the Musée des Beaux-Arts in Nantes.

Martin Ruzé; by Frans Pourbus the Younger, 1612 (No. 163; Passage to Picture Gallery)

211 HANS HOLBEIN the Younger (1497/8–1543)
A Young Man with a Pink
Holbein is chiefly known as portrait painter to the court of Henry VIII. A German, he made his first trip to England in 1526 at the invitation of Sir Thomas More. His second visit in 1532 lasted until his death from the plague in 1543. Holbein's English portraits are among his best works and are marked by a severe objectivity.

FRANCESCO GUARDI (1712–93)
Guardi was a Venetian painter of *vedute* (town views), mostly of Venice. Nos 230 and 231 are typical of the sort of painting he turned out by the hundred and which were sold as souvenirs to tourists. Comparison with the painting by Canaletto (No. 222, Main Staircase) highlights the differences between the two artists. Guardi's work is much less precise and has more atmosphere. It is easy to understand why Canaletto was generally preferred until the time of the Impressionists. In fact during his lifetime Guardi's pictures commanded only about half the price of Canaletto's.

228 *Pope Pius VI blessing the People of Venice*
This painting is altogether of a higher quality than Nos 230 and 231. It is one of a set of four paintings, commissioned to record the visit of the Pope to Venice on 15–19 May 1782. A large crowd is gathered in the Campo SS. Giovanni e Paolo, surrounding the Pope, who is addressing the people from a specially erected platform in front of the Scuola di S. Marco. On the right is the Colleoni monument and part of the church of SS. Giovanni e Paolo.

229 *A Study for a Crowd seen from behind*
Although this study, executed in pen and brush and black ink and wash, seems very close to No. 228, it is more likely to represent crowd scenes from another series painted by Guardi, depicting the Doge in the Bucintoro setting out for the Lido.

230 *The Dogana, Venice*
The Dogana is in the centre, with, on the right, S. Maria della Salute, and, on the left, the Church of the Redentore.

231 *S. Giorgio Maggiore, Venice*
The church and island of S. Giorgio Maggiore is on the left, with the point of the Giudecca on the right beyond the Canale della Grazia.

235 LORENZO LOTTO (*c.*1480–1556)
A Young Dominican Monk
Lotto's portrait subjects have a solid appearance, with a hard bright surface and intense colour. This portrait dates from early in Lotto's life, probably about 1506–8, when he was living near the Dominican friary of Recanati.

237 NORTH ITALIAN, *c.*1550
Odoardo Farnese
This small portrait is painted on slate and seems, from the cramped way the face occupies nearly the whole picture, to have been cut down from a larger work. It was previously catalogued as by Parmigianino but a more convincing attribution is to Niccolò dell'Abbate (*c.*1512–71), a Modenese painter who spent much of his life in France.

238 GIOVANNI DOMENICO TIEPOLO (1727–1804)
The Madonna appearing to St Anthony of Padua and St Francis of Paola
St Anthony, on the left, was a Franciscan noted for the purity of his life, hence the sprig of lily, an emblem of purity, on the steps below him. St Francis was the founder of the mendicant (begging) order of Minims. He kneels on the right with his attribute, the

Pope Pius VI blessing the People of Venice; by Francesco Guardi (No. 228; Passage to Picture Gallery)

sun, with the letters 'TAS' visible (the final letters of the word 'Charitas').

Domenico Tiepolo was the son and assistant of the more famous Giambattista Tiepolo. There are many similarities between the two artists, and the Upton picture was formerly attributed to Giambattista. Both were principally decorators, painting frescoes in churches and palaces in and around Venice and northern Italy. They also worked as far afield as Germany and Spain.

239 Tintoretto (Jacopo Robusti) (1518–94)
*The Wise and Foolish Virgins, c.*1548
Tintoretto was the last great Venetian artist of the 16th century. His major works were religious. He was a passionate and devout man who sought to bring out the emotional intensity of Biblical stories through a dramatic handling of light, gesture and form. When illustrating a story or parable, he always chose the most dramatic moment. It is not surprising then that he should have chosen that moment in this parable when the foolish virgins have just returned with new oil in their lamps but find the door locked against them. 'Let us in,' they cry. 'I do not know you,' replies the bridegroom, looking down from above, surrounded by the five wise virgins. The parable is a warning to be always prepared for the coming of the Son of Man, represented by the figure of the bridegroom; in the dramatic gestures of the foolish virgins we feel the despair of the damned.

255 El Greco (Domenikos Theotocopoulos) (1541–1614)
El Espolio (The Disrobing of Christ)
Signed in Greek
'Then the soldiers of the governor took Jesus into the common hall, and gathered unto him the whole band of soldiers. And they stripped him, and put on him a scarlet robe.' St Matthew, xxvii, 27–28.

El Greco ('The Greek') was born in Crete, but received most of his training in Venice. From 1577 he lived in Spain. His colour is startling, his figures elongated and there is a mystical intensity in his art.

The Bearsted picture is one of several smaller versions of the altarpiece in the sacristy of Toledo Cathedral (1577–9), which was his second major commission. Because of its high quality, it was probably a model for the altarpiece rather than a subsequent copy.

256 Madrid School, early 17th-century
(?) *St Elizabeth of Hungary*
Possibly a fragment from a larger painting.

The Picture Gallery

This room was added to the house in the 1927–9 alterations as a squash court and it still retains a small viewing balcony in the south-east corner. It was converted to its present use in 1936 to accommodate Lord Bearsted's collection of 15th- and 16th-century paintings.

Furniture

In the centre of the room is a large ***Italian walnut table*** dating from the 16th century. A ***French walnut buffet*** dating from the 16th century stands below the balcony; on the adjacent wall is a George III ***mahogany side-table***.

Pictures

143 Attributed to Hieronymus Bosch (*c.*1450–1516)
The Adoration of the Magi, Triptych
The paintings of Bosch have always invited interpretation but their meaning is largely hidden from us. They are a product of the twilight of Gothic imagination, and most of the symbolism behind these weird images lies buried in the Middle Ages. Bosch was not, however, an explorer of the unconscious mind or a member of some heretical sect. His paintings were owned by people of unimpeachable orthodoxy, such as Philip II.

We may still interpret some of the symbolism. In the centre panel, the collar of the second king is decorated with a scene showing the Queen of Sheba before Solomon; this was interpreted as a prototype of the Adoration. Similarly the orb carried by Balthasar, the Moorish king, is decorated with a scene depicting the Three Heroes offering water to David, another exemplar of the Adoration. The first king, Gaspar, is offering a sort of model.

Bosch was a moralist. He depicted the evil of the world to reform men from evil ways, but it is just that evil which is most vivid in his pictures: the disturbing half-naked man appearing at the door, who has been described by 20th-century interpreters as the Antichrist.

The right wing shows the mounted retinue of the kings, and the left wing Joseph collecting water to bathe Christ. When the wings are closed, they display a central roundel depicting Christ taken before Pilate after the Flagellation, with, below, grotesque demons painted in grisaille, resembling those from Bosch's paintings of Hell.

The Adoration of the Magi; attributed to Hieronymus Bosch (No. 143; Picture Gallery)

This is one of several versions of this composition painted by Bosch, the original of which is in the Prado, Madrid. The central panel is similar to the original, but the side panels are unique.

144 Attributed to AELBRECHT BOUTS (*c.* 1460–1549)
The Madonna and Child
Bouts was born in Louvain, where his father, Dirk Bouts, was employed as city painter, and there he worked in his father's workshop until the latter's death in 1475. Aelbrecht's work is in close imitation of his father's, but is somewhat clumsy and is often indistinguishable from workshop productions.

Follower of ROGIER VAN DER WEYDEN (*c.* 1399–1464)
145 *Christ and St John the Baptist*
St John is kneeling at Christ's feet beside the banks of the Jordan. The incident is explained by the verses from the Bible above their heads. These are in Dutch and were added to both Nos 145 and 146 at a later date. They read: above St John, 'I have need to be baptized of thee, and comest thou to me?'; and above Christ, 'Suffer it to be so now: for thus it becometh us to fulfil all righteousness.' Probably the right wing of an altarpiece, of which No. 146 is the corresponding panel.

146 *The Calling of Andrew and Simon Peter*
The first two disciples are taken by Jesus to his home, where the Virgin Mary is seated, sewing. The inscription in Dutch above Christ's head is now illegible, but the relevant passage from the Gospels is St John, i, 37–9: 'They came and saw where he dwelt, and abode with him that day.'

147 MASTER OF THE ST LUCY LEGEND (active late 15th century)
St Jerome in a Landscape, c. 1490
St Jerome (*c.* 340–420) is best known as the translator of the Scriptures into Latin, which afterwards became known as the Vulgate, the only authorised version of the Bible. He was a great scholar but, aware of the temptations of the scholarly life, he several times became a hermit. This is the meaning of the present picture. Jerome is seen kneeling in a much-torn soutane with his eyes fixed on the Crucifixion, while beside him lie his cardinal's cloak and hat, symbolising his cast-aside public life within the Church. Behind him in the landscape are incidents from his life. On the right are seen merchants, who,

after stealing an ass from a monastery, are being chased by a lion. On the left, the ass is returned to the monastery. The saint is accompanied by a lion, reflecting the legend that one became his faithful companion in the desert after he had removed a thorn from its paw.

The artist also enjoyed depicting the beauties of nature and the pleasures of life. The nettles and the dandelion leaves in the foreground have been carefully observed. In the distance is the city of Bruges (almost a signature of the Lucy Master), where, on the bridge between the two towers, a man stops to gaze into the water, while a woman is seen walking past. *St Jerome* is one of the finest of the Master's paintings.

148 Pieter Bruegel the Elder (*c.*1525/30–69)
The Death of the Virgin

Painted in grisaille, that is, in monochrome in a series of greys, probably to give an engraver a model to copy. It belonged to the famous geographer Abraham Ortelius (1527–98), who commissioned the engraving of it by Philip Galle in 1574.

The death of the Virgin takes place in a room at

(Left) St Jerome in a Landscape; by the Master of the St Lucy Legend (No. 147; Picture Gallery)

(Right) St John the Baptist and St Catherine of Alexandria; by the Master of the St Lucy Legend (No. 158; Picture Gallery)

night. She is sitting up in bed, receiving a lighted taper, probably from St Peter. The other disciples are kneeling behind, while, on the opposite side of the bed, Mary Magdalene smooths the Virgin's pillows. People are pushing forward into the room from a door at the rear, while St John is asleep by the fire. The picture is remarkable for being lit only by the fire and four candles, and though it appears very dark at first, the more we look, the more our eyes become accustomed to the dark and the more detail we see.

This is an unusual work for Bruegel, whom we associate with wide, bright landscapes populated by large numbers of peasants. It is quite a late work, possibly dating from 1564. As with No. 149, the Biblical story is treated as a contemporary event.

149 After PIETER BRUEGEL the Elder (*c.*1525/30–69)
The Massacre of the Innocents
It depicts the massacre of young children ordered by Herod following the birth of Christ. Bruegel situates it in a typical Flemish village, an intended criticism of the repressive Spanish forces then holding sway in the Netherlands. This is one of several contemporary copies of Bruegel's masterpiece, the original of which is in the Royal Collection at Hampton Court.

151 MASTER OF THE ST BARBARA LEGEND (active late 15th century)
A Man and his Wife
This portrait, probably painted about 1470, may once have formed the right-hand panel of a diptych; the other panel would have represented a sacred image, probably a Madonna and Child. The juxtaposition of the two images was an act of private piety. The person commissioning the painting is represented in an act of religious devotion.

The Master of the St Barbara Legend was an anonymous Flemish artist working in Brussels. He was a follower of Vrancke van der Stockt and a disciple of Rogier van der Weyden, both of whose names have previously been associated with this work.

153 GERARD DAVID (active 1484–1523)
The Madonna and Child
David was born in Oudewater in Holland but was in Bruges by 1484. His work, characterised by a delicate other-worldliness combined with a vivid attention to detail, marks the end of the Bruges School of Flemish painting.

154 Close follower of HUGO VAN DER GOES (d. 1482)
The Emperor Augustus's Vision of the Tiburtine Sibyl
According to tradition, the Madonna and Child appeared to Augustus and the Tiburtine Sibyl in a vision, and pointed out the site of the church of Santa Maria d'Aracoeli in Rome. The Madonna would in all probability have formed the companion panel of a diptych. The association of the pagan Augustus with the Madonna arose from the Messianic interpretation put on Virgil's 4th Eclogue, which led to his becoming a sanctified figure.

157 Attributed to the MASTER OF THE ST CATHERINE LEGEND (active late 15th century)
The Madonna and Child with an Angel
The artist is named after an altarpiece depicting that legend. He was a Flemish follower of van der Weyden. The Madonna is shown seated on the ground, an image known as the Madonna of Humility, and one much favoured by the Dominicans, who commissioned this picture. Two Dominican friars appear in the landscape.

158 MASTER OF THE ST LUCY LEGEND (active late 15th century)
St John the Baptist and St Catherine of Alexandria

The work of this anonymous Flemish artist shows the influence of Memling and van der Weyden, and is particularly notable for the elegance of the painting of his female saints and the richness of their costume: St Catherine's dress and richly embroidered crimson and gold robes, lined with ermine and studded with jewels, contrast with St John's robe and hair shirt.

St John is seen on the banks of the River Jordan; he is half turning to indicate where he is seen again baptising Christ in the river. It is not unusual to find in paintings of this period two stages of a story enacted within a single landscape. These pictures, hung here as a diptych, may once have formed the side panels of a triptych.

159 Attributed to the MASTER OF THE MAGDALEN LEGEND (active late 15th–early 16th century)
A Young Man wearing the Order of the Annunciation

This young man was thought to be Louis II, King of Hungary, because of the initials 'R. H.' on the scabbard of his dagger; the only other clue to his identity is the pendant, which is the Order of the Annunciation of the House of Savoy.

160 Attributed to the MASTER OF THE MAGDALEN LEGEND (active late 15th–early 16th century)
Philip the Fair (1478–1506)

Archduke of Austria, he was the son of Emperor Maximilian I (No. 213, Picture Gallery). The Master of the Magdalen Legend was a Flemish artist working in Brussels.

161 HANS MEMLING (*c.*1430/40–94)
An Unknown Man

A pupil of Rogier van der Weyden, he added an element of sweetness, but his religious paintings and portraits have the same qualities of restraint and calm. This painting was probably the right-hand wing of a diptych.

162 ? JOACHIM PATENIR (*c.*1480–1524)
The Temptation of Christ

Patenir was one of the first artists to devote himself to painting landscape. The figures in his pictures were usually painted by other artists, such as Quentin Massys and Joos van Cleve. Landscape was not yet a recognised genre of painting and still only provided the setting for the biblical, historical or portrait subject. In Patenir's paintings the stories are dominated by the landscape. Christ and the Devil are seen in two places at once: in the foreground, and also on top of the mountain peak where the Devil tempts Christ with 'all the kingdoms of the world'. Such a subject obviously suited Patenir's taste for extensive landscape, which typically changes from deep green in the foreground to a cool blue towards the horizon.

An Unknown Man; by Hans Memling (No. 161; Picture Gallery)

JAN PROVOOST (1462–1529)

Provoost came from Mons in the southern Netherlands, and first tried to establish himself as a painter in Antwerp. He was unsuccessful, and in 1494 his name appears as a master at Bruges. The spirit of his painting, however, is more akin to that of the progressive Antwerp school, influenced by Italian art, than the traditionalism of Bruges.

164 *The Virgin and St Joseph at Bethlehem*

The arrival of Joseph and Mary at Bethlehem is not often depicted in art. Provoost has treated it as a contemporary event with a characteristically red-brick Flemish house behind. The painting was

The Nativity at Night; by Jan Provoost (No. 165; Picture Gallery)

originally part of an altarpiece, probably the left wing of a triptych.

165 *The Nativity at Night*

167 Attributed to MICHAEL SITTOW (1469–1525)
The Nativity at Night
Although of Baltic origin, Sittow was a painter of the Flemish school. By 1482 we know he was in Bruges working with the Master of the St Lucy Legend (Picture Gallery, Nos 147, 158), and thereafter he seems to have been much in demand all over Europe. He worked in Spain, at the court of Queen Isabella of Castile, and England, in the service of Catherine of Aragon.

171 ROGIER VAN DER WEYDEN (*c.*1399–1464)
An Unknown Man
Van der Weyden was one of the great northern European artists of the 15th century, and a pioneer of portraiture. He was the pupil of Robert Campin in Tournai (1427–32), but after completing his apprenticeship he settled in Brussels, becoming City Painter in 1436. He visited Italy in 1450. In his own time Rogier achieved a great reputation and his influence on later artists was great. He built on the realistic achievements of Jan van Eyck but imbued his paintings with a deeper sense of feeling. This portrait, painted towards the end of his life, was probably the right-hand panel of a diptych, of which the other half would have been a Madonna and Child.

FRANÇOIS CLOUET (*c.*1510–72)
180 *Francis I of France* (1495–1547) *on Horseback*
Francis I succeeded his cousin, Louis XII, whose daughter he had married, in 1515. He appointed François Clouet court painter in 1541, on the death of the artist's father, Jean.

181 *Henry II of France* (1519–59) *on Horseback*
Second son of Francis I, he succeeded his father to the French throne in 1547. In 1533 he married Catherine de' Medici. The pendant of No. 180.

CORNEILLE DE LYON (*c.*1500/10–74)
182 *An Unknown Man*
Corneille, whose real name was Claude Corneille van de Cappelle, was born in The Hague but had settled in Lyons by 1533, where he was painter to Queen Eleanor. He was subsequently court painter to the Dauphin, then to King Henry II, and finally to King Charles IX. All the works associated with Corneille are portraits, and not surprisingly almost all are court portraits. However, none is signed, and as Corneille

ran a large workshop, attribution is very difficult. Corneille's portraits are small with a uniform background (usually green or blue), and a realistic, but courtly, elegance; the heads receive most attention, leaving the clothes rather summarily treated.

183 *An Unknown Man*
This portrait is of high quality and has more claim to being considered as by the hand of the master than No. 182.

184 JEAN FOUQUET (*c.*1420–before 1481)
St Michael slaying the Dragon
This fine miniature comes from a book of hours (private devotions) called *Les Heures d'Etienne Chevalier,* which was illustrated by Fouquet in 1452–60. It was unfortunately broken up in the late 18th century, but the majority of the leaves are now collected at the Musée Condé, Chantilly. Eleven leaves are still unaccounted for; the Upton leaf is the 45th. In the upper half St Michael is about to strike the seven-headed dragon, while below are scenes from Hell. In the centre of the picture is the device of Etienne Chevalier, with the letter 'M' denoting the antiphon of St Michael. A fragment of border illumination of a later date has been stuck to the picture, thus concealing the opening words of the antiphon: *Michael Archangelo, veni in adjutorium populi.*

Fouquet was the most important French painter of the 15th century. He was born in Tours but trained in Paris in the workshop of a miniaturist. His visit to Italy in the early 1440s was the first by a great northern painter. On his return to Tours in 1448, he was employed in the court of Charles VII. His work makes many references to his Italian trip: classical architectural detail, and an interest in anatomy, volume and perspective, some of which can be seen in this miniature.

185 Unknown
The Madonna and Child with Cherubim
This is a baffling painting. It has been variously described as Italian, French and German, and either dated around 1500 or dismissed as a fake on the basis of an analysis of the paint-surface. The situation is not clarified by a label on the reverse claiming it was in a sale in 1837, of which no record can be found. It is unusual, however, for a fake not to imitate the manner of any known artist.

192–203 FRENCH, *c.*1475–1500
A Series of Miniatures from the Story of Melusine
The story of Melusine, a fairy from French folklore, was first written down by Jean d'Arras in 1376. The twelve leaves on display here were taken from a manuscript of the late 15th century. They illustrate some of the adventures encountered by Melusine and her husband, Raymond of Poitiers.

St Michael slaying the Dragon; by Jean Fouquet (No. 184; Picture Gallery)

212 Attributed to MICHAEL PACHER (*c.*1435–98)
St George and the Dragon
Pacher was a Tyrolean painter and sculptor. In 1467 he is mentioned as the master of a shop making carved and painted wooden altarpieces in Bruneck, the leading artistic centre in the South Tyrol. The naturalistic quality of his painting suggests that he visited Italy, but his carved work always remained Gothic in spirit. The panel on which St George is painted is only 4mm thick, which suggests that it formed the shutter of an altarpiece, with another painting on the reverse and that at some stage the two were divided.

213 BERNHARD STRIGEL (1460/1–1528)
Emperor Maximilian I (1459–1519)
Son of Frederick III and Eleanor of Portugal, he was crowned Emperor of the Holy Roman Empire in

1508. The Hunts of Maximilian are the subject of the series of tapestries in the Hall.

Strigel was a German artist from the Swabian town of Memmingen, who was preferred by Emperor Maximilian I as his portrait painter, but the Upton painting does not seem to be of the quality associated with his work. It may therefore be by a member of his workshop.

214 YOUNGER MASTER OF THE SCHOTTEN ALTARPIECE (active *c.*1475–1500)
The Martyrdom of St Barbara

St Barbara was the daughter of a heathen named Dioscurus, who kept her locked up in a tower. During his absence on a journey, she had the two windows of her room made into three to represent the Trinity, and on her father's return confessed to him that she was a Christian. He took her before the Prefect, who had her tortured and she was later beheaded, her own father acting as executioner. In punishment for this barbaric act Dioscurus was struck by lightning on his way home and for this reason St Barbara is regarded as patron saint of thunderstorms, as well as protectress of miners and artillerymen. In art she is often placed beside a tower with three windows, which may be the gatehouse-tower that has three windows on this face.

Formerly catalogued as by Dürer's teacher, Michael Wolgemuth, this painting is now thought to be by the Younger Master of the Schotten Altarpiece, one of two artists deriving their names from the High Altar of the Schottenkirche in Vienna.

223 CARLO CRIVELLI (active 1457–93)
*Two Apostles, c.*1472

Crivelli was the elder and better of two Venetian artists (his brother was Vittorio) who were much influenced by the Paduan Mantegna. These two panels have been associated with the predella of an altarpiece from the church of the Franciscans at Montefiore dell'Aso, near Fermo, which was dismembered during the Napoleonic Wars.
The central panel, *The Dead Christ supported by two Angels*, is in the National Gallery, London.

224 Attributed to LAMBERT SUSTRIS (1515/20–95)
The Rape of Proserpine

Proserpine (Persephone) was the daughter of Zeus (Jupiter) and Ceres (Demeter). She was abducted by Pluto and taken to Hades, the kingdom of the underworld, where she was obliged to spend six months of the year (winter), returning to earth in the spring.

Sustris was born in Amsterdam, but worked all his life in Italy and Germany. He was much influenced by Titian and went with him to Augsburg in 1548.

Two Apostles; by Carlo Crivelli (No. 223; Picture Gallery)

225 Master of the Johnson Nativity (active *c.*1475–1500)
The Madonna and Child
This painting is a fragment from a larger work, possibly a *sacra conversazione* (the Madonna with other saints). The Master of the Johnson Nativity was a follower of Andrea del Verrocchio.

226 Master of the Fabriano Altarpiece (active mid-14th century)
The Last Supper
Christ is sitting at the left-hand end of the table with St John kneeling before him. He has just spoken the words: 'But, behold, the hand of him that betrayeth me is with me on the table.' Judas raises his hands in protest. The painting is in the late style of Giotto and must be by a member of his workshop.

227 Giovanni de Paolo (1403–83)
The Presentation of the Virgin
The young Virgin, with Zacharias and another priest, stands at the top of the steps leading to the golden tabernacle. She is turning to look down at St Anne. Behind St Anne are two fashionably dressed women. On the opposite side of the steps is Joachim. This panel would have formed part of the predella of an altarpiece, that is, part of a series of small panels beneath the main altar painting.

Giovanni di Paolo was, with Sassetta, the leading Sienese painter of the 15th century. Though his works show a knowledge of the discoveries of the early Renaissance in terms of perspective and design, his elegant figures are archaic and hark back to the 14th century.

232 North Italian, *c.*1300
Illuminated Initial 'D': Pentecost
This is a cutting from a choral book or other manuscript. It is painted on vellum and depicts eleven apostles, with SS. Peter and James in the centre, grouped within the initial. The Holy Ghost is represented as light breaking through the clouds.

233 Master of the Triumph of Chastity (active late 15th century)
The Madonna and Child with an Angel
The poor condition of this painting makes attribution somewhat difficult. In the past it has been variously described as the work of Filippino Lippi, or the studio of Botticelli, but it is now thought to be by the Master of the Triumph of Chastity, identified as Gherardo di Giovanni di Miniato (1446–97). It was painted about 1480.

234 Lombard, *c.*1470
Illuminated Initial 'S': Boyhood of Christ
A cutting from a choral book or other manuscript. Within the 'S' is seen the Holy Family: the Christ

The Presentation of the Virgin; by Giovanni di Paolo (No. 227; Picture Gallery)

Illuminated Initial 'S': Boyhood of Christ; Lombard School, c.1470 (No. 234; Picture Gallery)

Child is supported by the Virgin, left, and St Joseph, right; St Anne is standing behind the Virgin.

236 Follower of FRA FILIPPO LIPPI (*c.*1406–69)
Three Acts of Charity
The subject is taken from Matthew, XXV, 34–40, where Christ describes how on the Day of Judgement those who have acted charitably will be redeemed, for by so doing they will have acted charitably to Him. In the first scene, on the left, Christ, as the unknown stranger, is handed drink; in the second, he is handed food; and in the third, he is offered shelter.

The French Room

This is the only room on the ground floor which still preserves the dimensions of the 17th-century house. It is largely dedicated to French pictures.

Pictures

178 JEAN-BAPTISTE-JACQUES AUGUSTIN (1759–1832)
The Artist's Mother
Augustin was a miniaturist. He was largely self-taught and endured considerable hardship on first coming to Paris in 1781, but later became very popular, exhibiting at the Salon from 1791 to 1831.

179 After FRANÇOIS BOUCHER (1705–70)
Venus and Vulcan
Oil on papier mâché. This is probably a 19th-century copy of a painting by Boucher in the Louvre that was originally painted for Louis XV's bedchamber at Marly.

186 JEAN-BAPTISTE GREUZE (1725–1805)
The Head of a Girl

187 JEAN-BAPTISTE GREUZE (1725–1805)
A Child with an Apple

189 Attributed to JEAN-BAPTISTE GREUZE (1725–1805)
A Girl lying in Bed
At the beginning of his career Greuze made a name for himself as a painter of genre subjects extolling the virtuous poor, but later, to pay for his wife's extravagance, he began to paint pictures of scantily dressed young girls and others of mawkish sentimentality. The Upton paintings are characteristic examples of this kind of painting. Greuze died in poverty, unnoticed and embittered. This is the only one on canvas rather than a walnut panel and is the least convincing of the five.

Le Matin; by Jean-Baptiste Greuze (No. 191; French Room)

190 JEAN-BAPTISTE GREUZE (1725–1805)
A Girl holding a Spaniel

191 JEAN-BAPTISTE GREUZE (1725–1805)
Le Matin

204 ANTOINE VESTIER (1740–1824)
The Artist's Wife
Gouache on ivory
A successful portrait painter in oils, Vestier began his career by making enamel miniatures. He excelled in the rendering of materials, especially seen in portraits of women. He frequently painted his wife and children.

257 LUIS PARET Y ALCAZAR (1746–99)
The Quay, Olaveaga
Olaveaga is a suburb of Bilbao. This harbour scene is one of a number painted by the Spanish artist around 1783–8, when he was in exile in the north.

Porcelain

On either side of the fireplace are cabinets containing blue ground Worcester porcelain of the Dr Wall period (1751–74). A number of pieces show the blue scale ground typical of Worcester in this period, while the left-hand cabinet contains a tea-service in Sèvres style with exotic birds in gilt-bordered rococo panels on a mazarine blue ground (*c.*1770–80).

The West Stairs and First-Floor Landing

Pictures

6 Attributed to JOHN COLE (active 1720–44)
*A Flute Player, c.*1735
Signed *I. Cole*, probably the John Cole apprenticed to Tillemans in 1719. At the time this picture was painted, the German or transverse flute played by the sitter was a novelty, particularly favoured in amateur musical circles.

38 FRANCIS HAYMAN (1708–76)
*Two East Anglian Gentlemen with a Pointer, c.*1750–5
Hayman started his career painting scenes at Drury Lane theatre. He was best known for his designs for the decorations of Vauxhall Gardens in the 1740s, but his portrait groups in landscape settings, painted during the same period, influenced Gainsborough.

William Augustus Bowles as an American Indian Chief; by Thomas Hardy (No. 67; West Stairs)

45 JOHN HOPPNER, RA (1758–1810)
The Marquise de Sivrac and her Son
The Marquise de Sivrac was the daughter of Thomas Bonar of Camden Place, Chislehurst. He was a Russian merchant living in Paris who was murdered, together with his wife, by a footman in 1812. The Marquise had two children, one of whom we see here; both died young.

Hoppner was a portrait painter in the style of Reynolds. He achieved some eminence in the 1780s, when he was made portrait painter to the Prince of Wales, but he was eclipsed in later life by Sir Thomas Lawrence.

48 Sir THOMAS LAWRENCE, PRA (1769–1830)
William IV as Duke of Clarence
The Duke of Clarence (1765–1837), third son of George III, succeeded to the throne as William IV in 1830.

Lawrence was a precocious and largely self-taught artist who received his first royal commission in 1789 at the age of twenty. This portrait was probably painted between 1790 and 1795, at about the time Lawrence was made Painter-in-ordinary to the King (1792).

51 Ben Marshall (1767–1835)
A Farmer with a Horse and Cart
Signed and dated on the cart 'Farmer Marshall 09'

67 Thomas Hardy (1757–*c.*1804)
William Augustus Bowles (1763–1805) *as an American Indian Chief*
Bowles, as the unorthodox and romantic dress in which he chose to have himself painted suggests, was something of an adventurer. Cashiered from the British Army in North America, he took refuge with the Creek Indians. Although later reinstated, he was in England in 1790 as 'Chief of the Embassy from the Creeke and Cherokee Nations'. It may have been at this time that he sat for Hardy.

254 Eugenio Lucas y Padilla (1824–70)
The Sermon
This picture was previously attributed to Goya but it is almost certainly by the Spanish artist Lucas, who closely imitated his later style.

Una and the Lion, Chelsea (First-Floor Landing)

English porcelain

Two of the cabinets at the head of the West Stairs contain a selection of porcelain from the Chelsea factory. The third displays *Una and the Lion*, which was among the largest figures created by Chelsea. Una was one of the heroines in Edmund Spenser's poem *The Faerie Queene*, whose virtue was protected by a lion.

At the top of the stairs, turn right into the bedroom suite.

The Bedroom

This was originally a Chinese bedroom with green walls and red furnishings, created in the 1920s for Lady Bearsted by Morley Horder. Adjoining it were Lord Bearsted's dressing room and bathroom, which were much plainer than Lady Bearsted's suite of rooms. The bedroom is currently seen in a later form, with white walls and carpets, which was adopted in the late 1940s. It is hoped to return it to its former Chinese splendour.

Furniture

A black lacquer ***four-poster bed*** with silk bed-hangings dominates the room. However, the most spectacular is the view across the garden and estate that can be seen from the windows.

The Bathroom

The bold Art Deco style of this room is in marked contrast to the more restrained interiors in the rest of the house. It was created in the late 1920s by Morley Horder for Dorothy, wife of the 2nd Lord Bearsted, who had his own plainer and smaller bathroom. The pillars and window surrounds are lacquered in red, the skirting boards in black. The walls and vaulted ceiling are covered with aluminium leaf in imitation of more expensive silver leaf, which would have tarnished. The scheme may have been inspired by Lord Bearsted's brother-in-law, the interior designer Basil Ionides, who used silver-leaf decoration in a similar way in the auditorium of the Savoy Theatre in London. Morley Horder

(Left) The Bathroom

(Right) Bacino di S. Marco, Venice; by Canaletto, c.1725–6 (No. 222; Main Stairs)

made many sketches for the room, especially the light-fitting, which remains to be reproduced.

The decoration, which had been hidden beneath later layers of beige paint, has recently been reinstated by George Knibb & Sons.

The Corridor

Engravings

Either side of the corridor is a series of 18th-century prints, six of children engaged in various pursuits after A. de St Aubin, the remainder after Watteau, Pater, Moreau and others.

The Shell Exhibition

The bedrooms on the left of the corridor are devoted to an exhibition of posters produced by the Shell oil company in the 1930s, when its enterprising Publicity Director, Jack Beddington, commissioned many of the leading artists of the period to design for the company. Several other National Trust properties feature in the posters, including Bodiam Castle in Sussex and Brimham Rocks in Yorkshire. Rex Whistler's painting, *The Vale of Aylesbury*, above the chimneypiece in the second room, was also reproduced as a poster in a campaign to save this beautiful landscape from overdevelopment.

The Main Stairs

Pictures

103 JOHN WOOTTON (1682–1764)
A Classical Landscape with Animals
Wootton, often associated with equestrian portraits, also produced glowing classical landscapes such as this throughout his life. They were much sought after by gentlemen returning from the Grand Tour, who saw Wootton as an English Claude Lorrain. In consequence he was able to charge good prices and, unlike many artists of the day, lived very comfortably.

124 Follower of REMBRANDT (1606–69)
A Landscape with a Mill
Previously entitled *Rembrandt's Father's Mill*, as the mill itself appears in a Rembrandt etching of 1641, this landscape is now thought to be by a follower of Rembrandt, probably painted much later.

137 GERARD VAN HONTHORST (1590–1656)
Portrait of an Unknown Man
Following a stay in Italy, Honthorst became known as the 'Gherardo delle Notti' for his paintings of dramatic night scenes lit by single candles, but after a visit to England in 1628 he adopted a court style based on the painting of Van Dyck. In 1637 he was appointed court painter at The Hague and it is probably from this period that the portrait dates.

221 ALEXANDRE-JEAN NOEL (1752–1834)
Quinta de Benfica, Lisbon, 1780
The Neo-classical Quinta de Benfica near Lisbon was the property of the English Huguenot merchant Gerard de Visme (*c*.1755–98). This painting and two other views of the gardens were painted by Noel on a visit to Portugal in 1780.

222 CANALETTO (1697–1768)
*Bacino di S. Marco, Venice, c.*1725–6
This early picture by Canaletto gives a more extensive view than the eye could include in a single focus, and the artist probably made use of a *camera obscura* (a box containing lenses which enabled the artist to project an image of the view on to paper). It is a view looking towards the Doge's Palace and embraces the whole of the Venetian waterfront, bounded on the left by the entrance to the Canale della Giudecca and the Dogana, on the right by the steps and part of the façade of S. Giorgio Maggiore, and on the waterfront by the campanile of S. Zaccaria. Numerous gondolas and some bissone are collected round the Piazzetta, where the Doge's galley is moored. It has been suggested that the scene may represent the Feast of the Assunta at the moment when the Doge has departed for the Lido in the Bucintoro.

The garden

The garden front

This is much plainer and less baroque than the entrance front. The modesty of the central doorway is more in character with the dimensions of the original house, and may indicate the scale of architectural detailing on the entrance front before the additions of the 18th century. The lead rainwater heads bear the initials 'RC' and the date 1695.

Beyond Sir Rushout's house are two-storey bays at either end. The lower storeys were added by Francis Child, who bought Upton from William Bumstead in 1757, and their appearance can be seen in the painting by Devis in the Luggage Lobby. They added nothing to the dignity of the house, and Morley Horder wisely added the second storey to carry through the roof line and re-establish the symmetry.

History of the garden

Upton has a garden of great variety and historical interest. The garden shows evidence of the owners of the estate from its early history until the present day. The grotto in the Bog Garden, 'Monks Well', is so named because Upton was held in the 12th century by the canons of St Sepulchre's at Warwick. Tradition has it that a series of stewponds in the valley was created by the monks to supply fish for

the table. They would also almost certainly have grown vegetables. It is quite possible that the garden has been continuously cultivated ever since.

Sir Rushout Cullen made a considerable contribution to the layout of the garden. Late 17th-century gardens were invariably formal. The walls running down the east side and forming the southern boundary of the garden were part of his work. The large yews on the slope to the right of the lawn probably mark a series of terraces lined with clipped yew. He was also responsible for remodelling the stewponds to form a series of six regular rectangular ponds.

In contrast to this is Temple Pool. Enlarged by Robert Child in about 1775, it has an irregular outline typical of this period of landscape gardening. It can be glimpsed from Lady Bearsted's bedroom, but cannot be reached from the garden.

Until 1927 the garden's main purpose was to produce food: fruit, nuts, vegetables and fish for the house. From then onwards Lord and Lady Bearsted greatly improved the ornamental value of the garden. Much of the credit for both the design and the plantings must be given to Kitty Lloyd-Jones, who advised Lady Bearsted for many years, and to Tyrell Walker, the Head Gardener from 1920 to 1970. His high standards and accumulated knowledge of Upton made an invaluable contribution to the restoration and creation of the garden.

(Left) The garden front

(Right) The late 17th-century banqueting house in the Bog Garden was probably built by Sir Rushout Cullen

Tour of the garden

The terraces and lawn

The double terrace and balustrade on the garden front, designed by Morley Horder, replaced two grass banks and a number of formal Victorian beds. The upper terrace is planted with *Nepeta* × *faassenii* (Catmint) and *Rosa spinosissima* 'Williams Double Yellow', which was raised near Worcester in 1828 by John Williams.

The view from the terraces looks out across a large lawn framed on the right by cedars of Lebanon, and on the left by yews and pines which shelter a small rock garden. When one of the cedars fell a few years ago, the growth rings showed it to have been planted about 1740.

The valley gardens

The lawn appears to merge with the pasture-land on the slope opposite, but this is deceptive. At the far end of the lawn, hidden from the house, is a steep-sided valley which contains the bulk of the garden. This valley provides a wide range of growing conditions from the hot, dry terraces at the top to the pools and boggy borders in the bottom. The south-facing slope also provides ideal conditions for the vegetable garden which takes pride of place in the centre.

A new and fitting way into the valley was built for Lord Bearsted at the same time as the terraces were developed and replanted. This is the flight of dry-stone steps which lead down under the cedars at the south-west corner of the lawn.

The formal gardens

Below the steps are three formal gardens on the site of the 19th-century greenhouses and frame-yard. The Hibiscus Garden is planted with *Muscari comosum* 'Plumosum', *Viola* 'Maggie Mott', *Eryngium bourgatii*, *Hibiscus* 'Blue Bird' and *Crocus speciosus*, to give a succession of blue-toned flowers throughout the year.

Next is Lady Bearsted's Garden, planted in whites, pinks and purples, with a *Rosa perpetua* 'Felicia' forming a centrepiece. Below, surrounded by clipped yew hedges, is the Rose Garden, containing a selection of hybrid roses, with a statue of Pan in the centre.

The Bog Garden

At the base of the steps the valley turns to the right. This was the site of five of the medieval stewponds. The uppermost ponds had degenerated by 1927 into a marshy wilderness. This was developed during the 1930s into the existing Bog Garden. Dominated by three large *Cercidiphyllum japonicum*, it contains many plants which enjoy moist shade, including a variety of primulas, astilibes and irises. Throughout the summer the area is filled with luxuriant foliage: the contrasting shapes and colours of hostas, gunnera, rheums (ornamental rhubarb), bamboos and rodgersias.

The brick building at the end of the Bog Garden is a late 17th-century banqueting house probably built by Sir Rushout Cullen.

The Cherry Garden

On the site of another stewpond is the Cherry Garden; Japanese cherries are bounded on two sides by walls covered in fruit, and on the third by a nut plant, the whole area reflecting the productive origins of the garden. Indeed, the area was an extension of the vegetable garden until the 1950s, when a chequerboard pattern of pink *Prunus* 'Kanzan' and the white Double Gean *Prunus avium* 'Plena' was planted. The central cherries were killed when the pond flooded, leaving only the outer ring surviving. This is another area planned with the advice of Kitty Lloyd-Jones.

The Mirror Pool

The wall beside the pool is planted with vigorous herbaceous plants which appreciate the damp shady conditions. The plants here include the splendid giant yellow scabious *Cephalaria gigantea*, *Clematis* 'Wyvale' and *Ligularia przewalskii*.

The Wild Garden and Herbaceous Border

The Wild Garden is an informal area of specimen trees underplanted with spring bulbs, principally *Narcissus poeticus* (Pheasant Eye

The Bog Garden

daffodils). The wall separating the Wild Garden from the Herbaceous Border was until the 1930s the eastern boundary of the Kitchen Garden. The Herbaceous Border is colourful from early summer onwards, relying on large groups of plants including among many others Oriental Poppies, phlox, *Persicaria amplexicaulis*, aconitums and the magnificent two-metre-high *Rudbeckia* 'Herbstsonne'.

A path through the yew hedge behind the Herbaceous Border leads into the Kitchen Garden.

The Kitchen Garden

This is the very heart of the garden, and is still worked as a traditional English kitchen garden. There are long rows of all the vegetables one would expect to find in a garden supplying a large household, including such luxury crops as asparagus and globe artichokes. There is also a number of so-called 'unusual' crops, many of which are in fact old traditional vegetables that have recently found new popularity.

Below the vegetables lies a block of different varieties of soft fruit, including vineberries, loganberries and grapes.

The wall to the north provides a warm, sheltered position for some less hardy shrubs, for example *Drimys winteri*, *Hebe cupressoïdes* and *Myrtus communis* 'Tarentina'. Behind this is a wide border which contains representatives of

The Dry Bank

The Kitchen Garden

the National Council for the Conservation of Plants and Gardens reference collection of asters. There are cultivars of *Aster amellus*, *A. cordifolius* and *A. ericoïdes*, which bloom from July onwards. Phlox and delphiniums (some of which were introduced from America by Lord Bearsted) give colour earlier in the summer.

The terraces above contain plants enjoying warm, dry conditions. The lower one is dominated by Berberis hybrids and species; their flowers, leaves and berries make a display from early spring onwards. Above is a dry-stone wall retaining a shallow bank covered in aubretia, genistas, the prostrate ceanothus and other small shrubs. *Sisyrinchium striatum* makes a fine display at the foot of the wall during most of the summer. The wall above this terrace is the retaining wall to the lawn. It is predominantly covered by ceanothus, and the collection of Agapanthus and *Fuchsia* 'Thalia' at its foot is a good foil for the lavender hedge in the bed opposite. This area was extensively altered to its present form in the 1930s.

The Restaurant

This new, prominently sited building reflects the Statement of Significance recently prepared for Upton: it stipulates that the patrician 1920s feeling of well-being should pervade the whole of Upton House and its setting. The central frontispiece, making use of local stone from a quarry above Broadway, has the unusual feature of a 'floating frieze'. This part of the building is prompted by a miniature façade of about 1700 associated with the architect William Talman.

Early history of Upton

Though situated only a mile or so from the site of the Civil War battle of Edgehill (1642), Upton does not seem to have been touched by this, or for that matter, any great historical event. The changes it has witnessed have been of a more domestic kind. From its earliest history, Upton has been bought and sold many times, and successive owners have left their mark on its architectural character. Few written records survive and we often have to rely on our knowledge of the times to piece together its history.

Upton, as an area of land, is first mentioned when a member of the Arden family granted lands at Upton to the canons of St Sepulchre's at Warwick during the reign of Richard I (1189–99).

In the 14th century Upton gave its name to the family which held the land of the Ardens. In 1315 John de Upton is recorded as lord of the manor. This family remained at Upton until the reign of Henry VI (1422–71), when the estates passed to the Verneys of Wolford. After two further changes of ownership, the land was bought in the early 16th century by Sir William Danvers, in whose family Upton remained for the next 150 years. It seems likely that Danvers built a considerable house on the site, and a door in the basement of the present house may well be a relic of this building.

In 1688 Upton was bought by Sir Rushout Cullen for £7,000. Sir Rushout was the son of Sir Abraham Cullen, a London merchant of Brabant descent whose wife's family name was Rushout, hence the odd Christian name. Sir Rushout may have had pretensions to the status of country gentleman, as he pulled down the old house and by 1695 had built himself a house in the classical style. He had no heirs, and on his death Upton was bought by William Bumstead.

This winter view of Upton House from the south was painted about 1803 by Anthony Devis for the Child family, which then owned Upton. It shows the garden temple at the opposite end of the lake from its present position

Bumstead, who made minor alterations to the entrance front, seems to have been as much a figure of fun as his name suggests. He is remembered only through the correspondence of his neighbour, the eminent Gothick architect and squire of nearby Radway Grange, Sanderson Miller. The two men do not seem to have been the best of friends, for, as one of Miller's correspondents, Deane Swift, wrote, 'Pox take Bumstead and all fools who without cause are your enemies'. Financial difficulties continually beset Miller, and judging by comments in another letter, he may actually have had to contemplate selling up to the enemy: 'Could you find no other person as a purchaser of Radway than Mr Bumstead?', wrote Swift, 'I little thought that his prophecy wou'd so soon have been compleated.' Whatever the prophecy, Miller managed to stay on at Radway until his death in 1780, while Bumstead sold Upton in 1757 to the rich banker Francis Child.

For the Child family, and for the Earls of Jersey to whom the house passed by descent, Upton was a hunting-box and home to the heir to the title, their principal houses being at Osterley in Middlesex and Middleton Stoney in Oxfordshire. Several alterations were made both to the house and the garden, and it was sufficiently cared for to be the subject of a painting by Anthony Devis which hangs today in the Luggage Lobby (No. 14a).

The story of the descent from the Child family to that of the Earls of Jersey makes an interesting tale. Francis Child had a brother, Robert, whose daughter fell in love with an impoverished earl, the Earl of Westmorland. The Earl, knowing her father's antipathy to the match, eloped with the girl, hotly pursued by the irate father. By shooting the leading horse in Child's team, the couple escaped and were safely married at Gretna Green. But Child's wrath had the last word, for he cut his daughter out of his will, and left his immense fortune to the first child of the union, Lady Sarah Sophia Fane, who in 1804 married George, 4th Earl of Jersey.

Upton, as part of that inheritance, passed into the family of the Earls of Jersey, with whom it remained for most of the 19th century, until sold in 1894 to the 7th Earl of Chesham. It was sold again only four years later to Mr Andrew Motion, from whom it was bought in 1927 by Lord Bearsted.

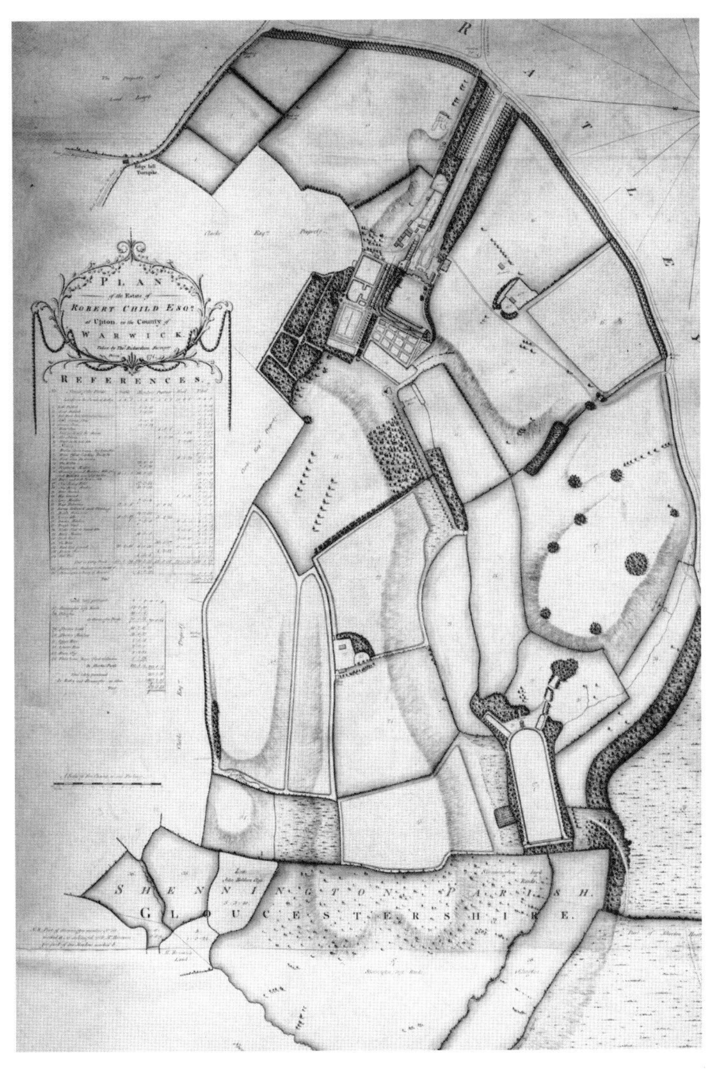

(Right) Plan of the Upton estate in 1774

Bibliography

ANON., 'Upton House', *Country Life*, 10 September 1904.

DICKENS, Lilian, and Mary Stanton, ed., *An Eighteenth-century Correspondence*, John Murray, 1910 [Bumstead].

DUGDALE, William, *Antiquities of Warwickshire*, 1656.

GORE, St John, *The Bearsted Collection: Pictures*, National Trust, 1964.

HENRIQUES, Robert, *Marcus Samuel*, Barrie & Rockliff, 1960.

LAING, Alastair, *In Trust for the Nation*, National Trust, 1995.

MALLET, J.V.G., *The Bearsted Collection: Porcelain*, National Trust, 1964.

OSWALD, Arthur, 'Upton House', *Country Life*, 5, 12 September 1936, pp. 248–53, 274–9.

SALES, John, 'Upton House', *Country Life*, 25 April 1991, pp. 66–9.

Acknowledgements

This guide is a revised version of that written by Simon Murray in 1989 and updated by Oliver Lane in 1995. It draws heavily on the 1974 edition by the late Gervase Jackson-Stops, and on the catalogues of the pictures (by St John Gore) and of the porcelain (by J. V. G. Mallet). The section on the garden was written by Sarah Cook, former Head Gardener at Upton, and revised by Heather Aston, present Head Gardener. I would also like to thank the following for their help: Julia Barker, Mike Booth, Anthony du Boulay, Jeffrey Haworth, Alastair Laing, Oliver Lane, Susan Newell and Henry Sandon.

Oliver Garnett, 2003

Registered charity no. 205846
ISBN 1-84359-051-4
Published by National Trust (Enterprises) Ltd

If you would like to become a member or make a donation, please telephone 0870 458 4000; write to The National Trust, PO Box 39, Bromley, Kent BR1 3XL; or see our website at: www.nationaltrust.org.uk

Illustrations: Guildhall Art Gallery/Corporation of London p. 4; National Trust p. 55; National Trust Photographic Library p. 54; NTPL/Matthew Antrobus pp. 8–9, 48, 49; NTPL/Michael Cooper p. 29; NTPL/Derek Croucher pp. 1 (bottom left), 5, 51, 52; NTPL/J. M. Dudley p. 12; NTPL/Andreas von Einsiedel p. 46; NTPL/Simon Folkes p. 36; NTPL/John Hammond pp. 1 (bottom right), 6, 27, 28, 30; NTPL/Angelo Hornak front cover, pp. 1 (top left), 2, 3 (left), 11, 13, 14, 16, 17, 20, 21, 22, 31 (bottom), 32, 33, 35, 37, 39, 40, 41, 42, 43 (top and bottom), 44, 47; NTPL/Christopher Hurst pp. 31 (top), 38; NTPL/Nadia Mackenzie pp. 1 (top right), 3 (top and bottom right), 7, 9 (bottom), 10, 15, 18 (top and bottom), 19 (top and bottom), 24 (left and right), 25, 26, 45; NTPL/Stephen Robson pp. 53, back cover.

Typeset from disc and designed by James Shurmer

Print managed by Centurion Press Ltd (BAS) for the National Trust (Enterprises) Ltd, 36 Queen Anne's Gate, London SW1H 9AS